Cracking the Code of Teen Behavior: Strategies for Communication and Connection

Sundvall Alan William

Published by Sundvall Alan William, 2024.

CRACKING THE CODE OF TEEN BEHAVIOR: STRATEGIES FOR COMMUNICATION AND CONNECTION

First edition. April 2, 2024.

ISBN: 979-8224707164

Written by Sundvall Alan William.

Table of Contents

Chapter 1: Understanding Teen Behavior

- INTRODUCTION TO TEEN development

Teen development, also known as adolescent development, is a crucial period of growth and change in an individual's life. Adolescence is typically defined as the period between childhood and adulthood, usually spanning from ages 10 to 19. This stage of life is marked by rapid physical, emotional, social, and cognitive development. It is a time of exploration, self-discovery, and identity formation as teens navigate the challenges and opportunities of transitioning from childhood to adulthood.

During the teenage years, adolescents undergo significant physical changes as they experience puberty. This period of growth is characterized by the development of secondary sexual characteristics, such as breast development in girls and the growth of facial hair in boys. Hormonal changes also play a key role in shaping physical development during adolescence, influencing mood, energy levels, and sexual desire. These physical changes can have a profound impact on a teen's self-image and self-esteem as they navigate the challenges of body image and societal expectations.

In addition to physical changes, teens also experience profound emotional changes as they navigate the complexities of their developing identity. Adolescence is a time of heightened emotional intensity, as teens grapple with issues of independence, autonomy, and social relationships. This period is marked by mood swings, conflicts with authority figures, and a strong desire for peer acceptance. As teens strive to establish their own sense of self, they may experiment with different identities, values, and beliefs, leading to a period of self-discovery and self-exploration.

Social development is another key aspect of teen development, as adolescents seek to establish and navigate relationships with their peers, family members, and other adults. Peers play a crucial role in shaping adolescent social development, as teens seek to establish their own social networks, form close friendships, and navigate the complexities of peer pressure. As teens strive for independence and autonomy, conflicts with parents and other authority figures may arise, as they seek to establish their own identity and assert their own values and beliefs.

Cognitive development is another important aspect of teen development, as adolescents undergo significant changes in their thinking, reasoning, and problem-solving abilities. During adolescence, teens begin to develop more advanced cognitive skills, such as abstract thinking, critical thinking, and decision-making. This period of cognitive development is marked by increased independence and autonomy, as teens strive to make their own decisions, solve their own problems, and take responsibility for their actions. During this time, teens undergo profound changes as they navigate the challenges of transitioning from childhood to adulthood. By understanding the complexities of teen development, parents, educators, and other adults can better support and guide adolescents as they navigate the challenges and opportunities of adolescence. By fostering a supportive and nurturing environment, adults can help teens navigate the complexities of identity formation, establish healthy relationships, and develop the skills and abilities they need to succeed in adulthood.

- Common challenges faced by teens in today's society

Today's teenagers face a myriad of challenges in navigating the complexities of modern society. One of the most common issues that young people encounter is the pressure to excel academically. With mounting expectations from parents, teachers, and society at large, teens often feel overwhelmed by the need to achieve top grades, excel in extracurricular activities, and secure a spot at a prestigious university. This pressure can lead to stress, anxiety, and burnout as teenagers strive to meet the high standards set for them.

Another challenge that many teenagers face is social media and its impact on their mental health. Platforms like Instagram, Snapchat, and TikTok have created a culture of comparison and competition among young people, where popularity and appearance are valued above all else. This constant exposure to curated images of perfection can erode self-esteem and breed feelings of inadequacy, leading to issues like depression and body dysmorphia. The pressure to maintain a flawless online persona can also create a sense of disconnection from reality and foster a fear of missing out on the seemingly perfect lives of their peers.

In addition to academic and social pressures, teenagers today also grapple with the pervasive influence of technology on their daily lives. The rise of smartphones, social media, and video games has blurred the boundaries between work and play, making it difficult for teens to unplug and unwind. This constant state of connectivity can disrupt sleep patterns, hinder personal interactions, and fuel addictive behaviors that detract from their overall well-being. The allure of screens and the instant gratification they provide can also distract teenagers from engaging in meaningful activities that promote personal growth and fulfillment.

Another challenge that plagues many teenagers in today's society is mental health issues. The pressures of academic success, social acceptance, and technological overload can take a toll on a young person's mental well-being, leading to conditions like anxiety, depression, and eating disorders. Unfortunately, stigma surrounding mental health still persists, making it difficult for teens to seek help and support when they are struggling. This lack of resources and understanding can exacerbate their mental health problems and prevent them from getting the help they need to thrive.

Furthermore, teenagers today face the daunting task of defining themselves and their identities in a rapidly changing world. With societal expectations and norms constantly in flux, young people are forced to grapple with questions of who they are, what they believe in, and where they fit in. This process of self-discovery can be fraught with confusion, insecurity, and loneliness as teenagers strive to find their place in a society that often feels alienating and indifferent. The pressure to conform to societal standards can stifle individuality and creativity, leading to a sense of disillusionment and disconnection from one's authentic self. As adults and educators, it is crucial that we listen to and support young people as they navigate these obstacles and strive to create a more inclusive and understanding environment for them to thrive. By acknowledging and addressing the unique challenges facing teenagers today, we can work together to foster a generation of resilient, compassionate, and empowered individuals who are equipped to navigate the complexities of the modern world.

- The impact of technology on teen behavior

Technology has become an integral part of the daily lives of teenagers around the world, drastically shaping their behavior and interactions with the world around them. From smartphones and social media to video games and virtual reality, technology has revolutionized the way teens communicate, learn, and entertain themselves. While these advancements have undoubtedly brought many benefits to the lives of teenagers, such as increased access to information and opportunities for social connection, they have also raised concerns about the potential negative impacts on teen behavior.

One of the most significant ways in which technology has influenced teen behavior is through changes in communication patterns. With the advent of smartphones and social media platforms like Instagram, Snapchat, and TikTok, teens now have a multitude of ways to connect with their peers in real-time. This constant connectivity has led to a shift in the way teens communicate, with many relying more on text messages and social media updates than face-to-face conversations. While this can facilitate quick and easy communication, it can also lead to a decrease in the quality of interpersonal relationships, as teens may prioritize online interactions over in-person connections.

Additionally, the widespread use of social media has had a profound impact on teen behavior in terms of self-esteem and body image. With platforms like Instagram and Snapchat often showcasing curated and edited versions of people's lives, teens can feel pressured to present an idealized version of themselves online. This can lead to feelings of inadequacy and comparison, as teens may measure their worth based on the number of likes and followers they receive. Furthermore, exposure to unrealistic beauty standards and photo-editing filters can contribute to body image issues and low self-esteem among teenagers, leading to a host of mental health concerns.

Technology has also had a significant influence on teen behavior in terms of academic performance and learning habits. While the internet provides a wealth of information at the fingertips of teens, it also poses challenges in terms of distractions and time management. With the constant allure of social media, video games, and online entertainment, many teens struggle to stay focused on their schoolwork and responsibilities. This can lead to a decline in academic performance and a lack of motivation to engage with traditional learning methods. Additionally, the prevalence of online resources and search engines has made it easier for teens to cheat and plagiarize, as they can quickly find answers to assignments with a simple Google search.

Furthermore, the rise of technology has transformed teen behavior in terms of leisure activities and entertainment preferences. Video games, virtual reality, and online streaming platforms have become ubiquitous in the lives of teenagers, offering endless opportunities for entertainment and escapism. While these digital experiences can be engaging and immersive, they also have the potential to become addictive and isolating, leading to a decrease in physical activity and social interaction. Many teens now spend hours on end playing video games or binge-watching TV shows, often at the expense of other important activities like exercise, homework, and face-to-face interactions. While technological advancements have undoubtedly enriched the lives of teenagers by providing new opportunities for communication, learning, and entertainment, they have also raised concerns about the potential negative effects on interpersonal relationships, mental health, academic performance, and leisure habits. It is essential for parents, educators, and policymakers to consider these impacts and work toward promoting a healthy balance between technology use and other aspects of teen life. By fostering open communication, setting boundaries, and encouraging critical thinking skills, we can help teens navigate the digital landscape in a responsible and mindful way.

Chapter 2: Effective Communication with Teens

- IMPORTANCE OF ACTIVE listening

Active listening is a crucial skill that plays a significant role in communication and interpersonal relationships. It involves not only hearing the words that are being spoken but also understanding the underlying message, emotions, and intentions behind them. Active listening requires full attention, focus, and engagement with the speaker, showing them that you are genuinely interested in what they have to say.

One of the key reasons why active listening is important is that it promotes better understanding and comprehension. When we actively listen to someone, we are able to grasp the context, nuances, and subtleties of their message, allowing us to respond appropriately and effectively. This is essential in both personal and professional settings, as it helps to avoid misunderstandings, conflicts, and miscommunications that can arise from misinterpreting or misjudging the speaker's words.

Furthermore, active listening fosters empathy and emotional intelligence. By paying attention to the speaker's tone of voice, body language, and facial expressions, we can better understand their feelings, thoughts, and perspectives. This allows us to connect with them on a deeper level, showing them that we care about their well-being and are willing to support them in their challenges and concerns. Empathy is a powerful tool in building trust, rapport, and collaboration in relationships, as it demonstrates our ability to acknowledge and validate the other person's experiences and emotions.

In addition, active listening enhances problem-solving and decision-making skills. By actively listening to different viewpoints, ideas, and opinions, we can gather diverse perspectives and insights that can help us make informed and well-rounded decisions. This is particularly important in the workplace, where complex issues and challenges often require a collaborative and multidimensional approach. By listening actively and openly to others, we can leverage the collective intelligence and creativity of the team, leading to more innovative and effective solutions.

Moreover, active listening promotes learning and personal growth. When we listen attentively to others, we have the opportunity to expand our knowledge, broaden our perspective, and deepen our understanding of diverse topics and subjects. This not only enriches our intellectual and emotional intelligence but also helps us develop a growth mindset and a lifelong learning attitude. By engaging in active listening, we can continuously improve our communication skills, critical thinking, and problem-solving abilities, making us more adaptable and resilient in facing the challenges and complexities of the modern world. By actively listening to others, we can foster better relationships, enhance communication, and promote empathy, understanding, and collaboration. In an increasingly interconnected and diverse world, active listening is an invaluable tool that can help us navigate the complexities and uncertainties of our personal and professional lives, fostering mutual respect, trust, and cooperation among individuals and communities.

- Setting boundaries and expectations

Setting boundaries and expectations is a crucial aspect of maintaining healthy relationships, both personally and professionally. By clearly defining our limits and communicating our needs and desires, we create a framework that fosters respect, mutual understanding, and trust. Without boundaries and expectations, conflicts can arise, misunderstandings can occur, and individuals may feel taken advantage of or overwhelmed. In this essay, we will explore the importance of setting boundaries and expectations, how to establish them effectively, and the benefits of doing so in various contexts.

One of the key reasons why setting boundaries and expectations is essential is that it helps us maintain our autonomy and self-respect. When we clearly communicate our needs and limits to others, we are asserting our right to be treated with respect and consideration. By setting boundaries, we are showing others how we expect to be treated, which can prevent misunderstandings and conflicts from arising. Moreover, by setting expectations, we are establishing a shared understanding of what is acceptable behavior and what is not, which can help us avoid unnecessary tension or stress in our relationships.

In addition to preserving our autonomy and self-respect, setting boundaries and expectations can also help us protect our emotional and mental well-being. When we establish clear boundaries with others, we are defining what is and is not acceptable in terms of our personal space, time, and energy. By doing so, we are creating a safe and healthy environment for ourselves where we can thrive and grow. Setting expectations can also help us manage our own expectations of others, avoiding disappointment or frustration when our needs are not met. By setting realistic and achievable expectations, we can reduce the likelihood of feeling let down or betrayed by others.

Furthermore, setting boundaries and expectations can improve our communication skills and strengthen our relationships with others. When we clearly communicate our boundaries and expectations, we are promoting open and honest communication with others. By expressing our needs and desires in a respectful and assertive manner, we are creating a space for dialogue and negotiation that can lead to greater understanding and compromise. In addition, by setting boundaries and expectations, we are building trust and respect with others, as they will see us as someone who values their own well-being and respects the boundaries of others.

To establish boundaries and expectations effectively, it is important to first identify our own needs and limits. This requires self-reflection and introspection to understand what is important to us and what we are willing to tolerate. Once we have a clear understanding of our own boundaries and expectations, we can begin to communicate them to others. This may involve setting clear and specific boundaries with specific individuals or groups, such as family members, friends, or coworkers. It may also involve setting boundaries with ourselves, such as limiting our exposure to negative influences or setting aside time for self-care and relaxation.

When communicating our boundaries and expectations to others, it is important to do so in a clear, respectful, and assertive manner. It is important to use "I" statements to express our own feelings and needs, rather than blaming or criticizing others. For example, instead of saying, "You always make me feel stressed out," we can say, "I feel stressed out when there is too much on my plate. " This helps others understand our perspective and encourages them to respond in a more compassionate and understanding way. It is also important to be consistent and firm in enforcing our boundaries and expectations, even if it means setting consequences for those who violate them.

Setting boundaries and expectations can have numerous benefits in various contexts, from personal relationships to professional settings. In personal relationships, setting boundaries can help us protect our emotional well-being and maintain healthy boundaries with others. For example, setting boundaries with friends and family members can help us maintain a healthy balance between our own needs and the needs of others, preventing us from feeling overwhelmed or taken advantage of. In romantic relationships, setting boundaries can help us establish mutual respect and trust, creating a strong foundation for a healthy and fulfilling partnership.

In professional settings, setting boundaries and expectations can help us establish clear guidelines for behavior and performance, enabling us to work more effectively with others. For example, setting expectations with coworkers can help us clarify our roles and responsibilities within a team, facilitating collaboration and productivity. Setting boundaries with supervisors and subordinates can also help us navigate power dynamics and maintain a professional demeanor in the workplace. By setting boundaries and expectations in our professional lives, we can create a more positive and harmonious work environment for ourselves and our colleagues. By clearly defining our limits and needs, we create a framework for respectful and understanding interactions with others. By setting expectations, we establish shared understanding and respect for what is acceptable behavior and what is not. In personal relationships, setting boundaries can help us protect our emotional well-being and maintain healthy relationships with others. In professional settings, setting boundaries and expectations can help us establish clear guidelines for behavior and performance, enabling us to work more effectively with others.

- Strategies for promoting open communication

Effective communication is a crucial component of organizational success, as it facilitates collaboration, transparency, and understanding among team members. Open communication fosters a culture of trust and respect, allowing employees to freely share ideas, concerns, and feedback. In order to promote open communication in the workplace, organizations must implement strategies that create a supportive and inclusive environment where employees feel comfortable expressing themselves.

One strategy for promoting open communication is to establish clear and consistent channels for sharing information. This could include regular team meetings, email updates, and intranet platforms where employees can access important announcements and updates. By making information readily available and easily accessible, organizations can ensure that employees are informed and engaged in the decision-making process. Additionally, having a designated point person or team responsible for communication can help streamline the flow of information and ensure that messages are being effectively communicated to all relevant stakeholders.

Another important strategy for promoting open communication is to actively encourage feedback and input from employees. This can be done through regular surveys, suggestion boxes, or open-door policies that allow employees to share their thoughts and ideas with management. By creating opportunities for employees to provide feedback, organizations can gain valuable insights into the needs and concerns of their workforce, and demonstrate that their opinions are valued and respected. Additionally, feedback mechanisms can help identify areas for improvement and foster a culture of continuous learning and growth within the organization.

In order to promote open communication, organizations must also prioritize active listening and empathy. This means taking the time to truly listen to what employees have to say, and demonstrating understanding and compassion towards their perspectives. By actively listening to employee concerns and feedback, organizations can build trust and rapport with their workforce, and create a sense of psychological safety that encourages open and honest communication. Additionally, practicing empathy can help managers and leaders better understand the motivations and emotions behind employee communication, and respond with sensitivity and compassion.

Creating a culture of open communication also requires setting clear expectations and guidelines for communication within the organization. This could include establishing communication norms, such as responding to emails within a certain timeframe, or using specific communication channels for different types of messages. By setting clear expectations for communication, organizations can avoid misunderstandings and conflicts, and ensure that information is being communicated effectively and efficiently. Additionally, providing training and resources on effective communication techniques can help employees develop the skills and confidence they need to communicate openly and effectively with their colleagues.

In order to successfully promote open communication, organizations must also be willing to address and resolve conflicts that may arise. Conflict is a natural part of human interaction, and can actually be a catalyst for positive change and growth within an organization. However, unresolved conflicts can lead to resentment, mistrust, and decreased morale among employees. By creating a safe and supportive environment for addressing conflict, organizations can encourage open and honest communication, and empower employees to raise concerns and work towards resolution in a constructive manner. This could include implementing conflict resolution training, providing mediation services, or establishing clear protocols for addressing and resolving conflicts within the organization. By establishing clear communication channels, encouraging feedback and input from employees, prioritizing active listening and empathy, setting clear expectations and guidelines for communication, and addressing conflicts in a constructive manner, organizations can create a culture of open communication that fosters collaboration, innovation, and success. By prioritizing open communication, organizations can build stronger relationships with their employees, increase engagement and productivity, and create a supportive and inclusive work environment where all voices are heard and valued.

Chapter 3: Building Trust and Connection

- CREATING A SUPPORTIVE environment for teens

Creating a supportive environment for teens is essential for their overall well-being and development. During adolescence, young people go through significant physical, emotional, and cognitive changes that can leave them feeling overwhelmed and vulnerable. As parents, educators, and caregivers, it is crucial to provide a safe space where teens feel understood, respected, and empowered to navigate the challenges they face. By fostering an environment that encourages open communication, promotes positive relationships, and offers guidance and resources, we can help teenagers thrive during this critical stage of their lives.

One of the key components of a supportive environment for teens is effective communication. Adolescents often struggle with expressing their thoughts and emotions, which can lead to misunderstandings and conflicts with adults and peers. By creating opportunities for open and honest dialogue, we can help teens feel heard and valued. This can involve actively listening to their concerns, validating their experiences, and offering guidance and support without judgment. By building trust and rapport with teens, we can establish a foundation for healthy communication that will benefit them throughout their lives.

In addition to communication, positive relationships play a crucial role in creating a supportive environment for teens. Adolescence is a time when young people are exploring their identities and seeking connection with others. By fostering healthy relationships with family members, friends, and mentors, we can help teens feel supported and accepted. Encouraging empathy, compassion, and respect in these relationships can also promote emotional intelligence and social skills that will serve teens well in their interactions with others.

Furthermore, providing opportunities for teens to engage in meaningful activities and form connections with peers who share their interests can enhance their sense of belonging and self-esteem.

Guidance and resources are also important components of a supportive environment for teens. Adolescents are faced with a myriad of challenges, ranging from academic pressures to peer conflicts to mental health issues. By offering guidance and resources that address these challenges, we can help teens navigate difficult situations and make informed decisions. This can involve providing information on mental health resources, academic support services, and healthy coping strategies for managing stress and anxiety. By equipping teens with the tools they need to overcome obstacles and build resilience, we can empower them to take control of their lives and reach their full potential. By fostering open dialogue, building healthy relationships, and offering support and guidance, we can help teens navigate the challenges of adolescence and develop the skills they need to thrive. As adults, it is our responsibility to create a safe and nurturing environment that empowers young people to grow, learn, and become confident individuals. By investing in the well-being of teens, we can contribute to a brighter future for them and for society as a whole.

- Establishing rapport and trust

Establishing rapport and trust is a crucial aspect of building successful relationships, whether in personal or professional settings. In order to establish rapport and trust, it is important to demonstrate empathy, active listening, and genuine interest in the other person. By showing that you are attentive and open-minded, you can create a positive and welcoming environment that encourages others to feel comfortable and share their thoughts and feelings.

One of the key components of establishing rapport and trust is empathy. Empathy is the ability to understand and share the feelings of another person. When you demonstrate empathy towards others, you show that you care about their well-being and are willing to take their perspective into consideration. By acknowledging and validating their emotions, you create a sense of connection and understanding that can help to build trust. Empathy also fosters a sense of goodwill and mutual respect, as it shows that you are willing to invest the time and effort to truly understand the other person's point of view.

Active listening is another essential skill in establishing rapport and trust. Active listening involves giving your full attention to the speaker, maintaining eye contact, and offering verbal and non-verbal cues to show that you are engaged and interested in what they have to say. By demonstrating that you are actively listening, you can make the other person feel heard and valued, which can help to build trust and strengthen the relationship. Active listening also helps to clarify misunderstandings and ensure that both parties are on the same page, leading to more effective communication and collaboration.

In addition to empathy and active listening, demonstrating genuine interest in the other person is key to establishing rapport and trust. Genuine interest involves showing curiosity and openness towards the other person's thoughts, opinions, and experiences. By asking thoughtful questions and seeking to learn more about the other person, you can demonstrate that you value their perspective and are interested in building a meaningful connection. Genuine interest also helps to create a sense of reciprocity, as the other person is more likely to reciprocate your interest and engage in the interaction in a positive and meaningful way. By demonstrating empathy, active listening, and genuine interest in the other person, you can create a positive and welcoming environment that fosters connection and understanding. Building rapport and trust takes time and effort, but the rewards of stronger relationships, increased collaboration, and enhanced communication are well worth it. By prioritizing empathy, active listening, and genuine interest in your interactions with others, you can create a foundation of trust and rapport that will serve you well in all aspects of your life.

- Encouraging teens to express their feelings and thoughts

Encouraging teens to express their feelings and thoughts is crucial for their emotional development and well-being. In today's fast-paced and technology-driven world, teenagers are often bombarded with distractions and pressures that can make it difficult for them to connect with their emotions and communicate effectively. By creating a safe and supportive environment where teens feel free to express themselves, adults can help them navigate the challenges of adolescence and build strong emotional intelligence skills.

One of the key ways to encourage teens to express their feelings and thoughts is by actively listening to them without judgment. It is important for adults to make an effort to truly understand where teens are coming from and validate their experiences, even if they may not always agree with them. By showing empathy and openness, adults can create a space where teens feel comfortable sharing their innermost thoughts and feelings without fear of being criticized or dismissed.

Another important aspect of encouraging teens to express their feelings and thoughts is to model healthy communication skills. Adults can lead by example by demonstrating effective ways of expressing emotions, such as using "I" statements and active listening techniques. By showing teens how to communicate assertively and respectfully, they can help them develop the confidence to express themselves in a constructive manner.

Encouraging teens to express their feelings and thoughts also involves teaching them how to manage their emotions in a healthy way. This includes helping them identify and label their feelings, as well as providing them with coping strategies to deal with stress and difficult emotions. By equipping teens with the tools they need to regulate their emotions, adults can empower them to navigate the ups and downs of adolescence with resilience and self-awareness.

In addition to individual support, adults can also create opportunities for teens to express themselves through group activities and discussions. Teenagers often benefit from interacting with their peers and sharing their experiences in a supportive and non-judgmental environment. By fostering a sense of community and belonging, adults can help teens build meaningful connections and develop the social skills necessary to communicate effectively with others. By providing them with a safe and supportive space to share their emotions and experiences, adults can help teens develop the emotional intelligence skills they need to navigate the complexities of adolescence and thrive in today's fast-paced world. Through active listening, modeling healthy communication skills, teaching emotional regulation techniques, and creating opportunities for peer support, adults can empower teens to express themselves authentically and develop the confidence to navigate the ups and downs of adolescence with resilience and self-awareness.

Chapter 4: Dealing with Conflict

- MANAGING CONFLICT in a constructive manner

Conflict is an inevitable part of human interactions, both in personal and professional settings. It arises when individuals have different perspectives, needs, or values. While conflict can sometimes be uncomfortable or challenging, it can also be an opportunity for growth, learning, and strengthening relationships. Managing conflict in a constructive manner is essential for maintaining a positive and productive work environment, fostering collaboration and innovation, and promoting overall well-being.

One of the key principles of managing conflict in a constructive manner is effective communication. Clear and open communication is essential for understanding the root causes of conflict, expressing needs and concerns, and finding mutually agreeable solutions. Active listening is a crucial component of effective communication, as it allows individuals to truly understand others' perspectives and emotions. By listening attentively and empathetically, individuals can show respect and build trust, which are essential for resolving conflicts in a positive and constructive manner.

Another important aspect of managing conflict in a constructive manner is maintaining a positive attitude and mindset. Rather than seeing conflict as something negative or destructive, individuals can reframe it as an opportunity for growth, learning, and improvement. By approaching conflict with a positive attitude, individuals can stay calm, focused, and solution-oriented, rather than becoming defensive, adversarial, or aggressive. Maintaining a positive mindset also involves being open-minded, flexible, and willing to consider alternative perspectives and solutions.

In addition to effective communication and a positive attitude, conflict resolution skills are also essential for managing conflict in a constructive manner. These skills include problem-solving, negotiation, compromise, and collaboration. Problem-solving involves identifying the root causes of conflict, brainstorming possible solutions, and evaluating their feasibility and effectiveness. Negotiation involves finding common ground and reaching mutually acceptable agreements. Compromise involves making concessions and finding middle ground, while collaboration involves working together to achieve shared goals and objectives.

Furthermore, emotional intelligence is a critical skill for managing conflict in a constructive manner. Emotional intelligence involves recognizing, understanding, and managing emotions in oneself and others. By being aware of one's own emotions and triggers, individuals can respond to conflict in a calm, rational, and assertive manner, rather than reacting impulsively, emotionally, or defensively. By also being empathetic and understanding others' emotions and perspectives, individuals can build rapport, trust, and mutual respect, which are essential for resolving conflicts in a positive and constructive manner.

Moreover, creating a culture of respect, trust, and psychological safety is crucial for managing conflict in a constructive manner. When individuals feel respected, valued, and heard, they are more likely to communicate openly and honestly, express their needs and concerns, and work together to find mutually acceptable solutions. Trust is also essential for conflict resolution, as it provides a foundation for open communication, collaboration, and relationship-building. Psychological safety involves creating an environment where individuals feel comfortable taking risks, expressing their thoughts and feelings, and challenging the status quo, without fear of judgment, retaliation, or retribution. By practicing effective communication, maintaining a positive attitude and mindset, developing conflict resolution skills, and cultivating emotional intelligence, individuals can navigate conflict in a positive and constructive manner. By also creating a culture of respect, trust, and psychological safety, organizations can create environments where conflict is viewed as an opportunity for growth, learning, and strengthening relationships. Ultimately, by managing conflict in a constructive manner, individuals and organizations can achieve better outcomes, build stronger connections, and create more positive and fulfilling work environments.

- Understanding the root causes of teen behavior

Understanding the root causes of teen behavior is a complex and multifaceted topic that requires a deep exploration of various factors that contribute to adolescent actions. Teen behavior is influenced by a combination of biological, psychological, social, and environmental factors that interact in dynamic ways to shape how young people think, feel, and act. By studying the root causes of teen behavior, researchers and practitioners can develop more effective strategies for supporting adolescents as they navigate the challenges of adolescence and build the foundation for healthy development and well-being.

One of the key factors influencing teen behavior is the biological changes that occur during adolescence. Adolescents undergo significant physical and hormonal changes that affect their mood, cognition, and behavior. The onset of puberty triggers a surge in hormones, such as testosterone and estrogen, which can impact mood regulation, impulse control, and decision-making skills. These biological changes can contribute to mood swings, risk-taking behavior, and heightened emotional reactivity in teens. Understanding the neurobiological processes that underlie these changes can provide valuable insights into why teens behave the way they do and how best to support their development.

In addition to biological factors, psychological factors also play a crucial role in shaping teen behavior. Adolescents are in the process of developing their identity, autonomy, and sense of self, which can lead to conflicts with parents, teachers, and other authority figures. The quest for independence and self-expression can manifest in rebellious behavior, defiance of rules, and experimentation with risky behaviors. Teens may also grapple with issues of self-esteem, body image, and social acceptance, all of which can influence their behavior and decision-making. By understanding the psychological processes that underlie these issues, adults can offer support and guidance to help teens navigate the turbulent waters of adolescence more effectively.

Social influences also play a significant role in shaping teen behavior. Adolescents are highly attuned to the opinions and behaviors of their peers, and social pressures can have a profound impact on their choices and actions. Peer pressure, social norms, and media influences can all contribute to risky behaviors, such as substance abuse, delinquency, and early sexual activity. In addition, family dynamics, parental expectations, and community resources can also influence teen behavior. By examining the social contexts in which teens live and interact, researchers can gain a better understanding of how social influences shape adolescent behavior and how to promote positive social connections and support networks for young people.

Environmental factors, such as poverty, discrimination, and violence, can also have a significant impact on teen behavior. Adolescents who grow up in unstable or unsafe environments may be more likely to engage in problem behaviors as a way of coping with stress and trauma. Exposure to violence, abuse, or neglect can have long-lasting effects on mental health and behavior, leading to issues such as aggression, depression, and substance abuse. By addressing the environmental factors that contribute to teen behavior problems, policymakers and community leaders can create safer, more supportive environments for young people to thrive and grow. By examining the interplay of these factors, researchers and practitioners can gain valuable insights into why teens behave the way they do and how best to support their health, well-being, and success. By addressing the root causes of teen behavior, we can create a more nurturing and supportive environment for young people to thrive and reach their full potential.

- Strategies for resolving conflicts peacefully

Conflict is a natural part of human interaction and can arise in a variety of situations, both personal and professional. However, resolving conflicts peacefully is essential for maintaining positive relationships and fostering a positive work or social environment. There are several strategies that can be employed to resolve conflicts peacefully, and understanding these strategies can help individuals navigate difficult situations with grace and tact.

One important strategy for resolving conflicts peacefully is active listening. This involves giving the other party your full attention and truly trying to understand their perspective. By listening carefully to what the other person is saying, you can gain insight into their feelings and motivations, which can help you find common ground and come to a resolution. Active listening also involves asking clarifying questions and paraphrasing what the other person has said to ensure that you have understood their position correctly. This demonstrates to the other party that you are committed to resolving the conflict in a respectful and constructive manner.

Another key strategy for resolving conflicts peacefully is maintaining open and honest communication. Often, conflicts arise due to misunderstandings or miscommunications, so it is important to be clear and direct in your communication with the other party. Avoiding passive-aggressive behaviors or making assumptions about the other person's intentions can help prevent conflicts from escalating. Instead, focus on expressing your thoughts and feelings in a calm and non-confrontational manner, and encourage the other person to do the same. By fostering open communication, you can create a safe space for discussing the issues at hand and finding mutually agreeable solutions.

It is also important to practice empathy and understanding when resolving conflicts peacefully. Put yourself in the other person's shoes and try to see the situation from their perspective. Consider what emotions or concerns may be driving their actions, and strive to validate their feelings even if you do not agree with their behavior. Showing empathy towards the other party can help build trust and rapport, which is essential for reaching a resolution that satisfies everyone involved. By demonstrating compassion and understanding, you can create a cooperative atmosphere in which both parties feel heard and respected.

In addition to active listening, open communication, and empathy, compromise is another important strategy for resolving conflicts peacefully. Compromise involves finding common ground and working towards a solution that meets the needs and interests of both parties. This may require both parties to make concessions and be willing to collaborate in finding a resolution that is fair and equitable. By being open to compromise, you can demonstrate your willingness to work towards a mutually beneficial outcome and show that you value the relationship with the other party. Compromise is a key component of conflict resolution and can help prevent conflicts from escalating into more serious disputes.

Lastly, seeking the assistance of a neutral third party can be a helpful strategy for resolving conflicts peacefully. In some cases, conflicts may be too complex or emotionally charged to resolve on one's own, and the intervention of a mediator or facilitator may be necessary. A neutral third party can help facilitate communication between the conflicting parties, clarify misunderstandings, and guide the conversation towards a resolution.

Mediation can be particularly useful in cases where there is a power imbalance or when emotions are running high, as the mediator can provide a neutral perspective and help both parties find common ground. By seeking outside help, you can increase the likelihood of reaching a peaceful resolution and maintaining positive relationships moving forward. By employing strategies such as active listening, open communication, empathy, compromise, and seeking the assistance of a neutral third party, individuals can work towards resolving conflicts in a constructive, respectful, and collaborative manner. By fostering understanding, cooperation, and mutual respect, individuals can create a positive and harmonious environment in which conflicts are addressed and resolved in a peaceful and effective way. Ultimately, the ability to resolve conflicts peacefully is a valuable skill that can help individuals build strong and positive relationships both personally and professionally.

Chapter 5: Promoting positive self-esteem

- THE IMPORTANCE OF self-esteem in teen development

Self-esteem is a crucial component of adolescent development, as it plays a significant role in shaping a teenager's sense of self-worth and overall well-being. Defined as the belief in one's own abilities and worth, self-esteem is a fundamental aspect of psychological health and personality development. In adolescence, self-esteem undergoes significant changes as teenagers navigate the challenges of identity formation, social relationships, academic achievement, and physical changes. During this critical period of growth and self-discovery, it is essential for teenagers to develop a healthy level of self-esteem to navigate the complexities of adolescence and build a strong foundation for future success and well-being.

One of the key reasons why self-esteem is important in teen development is its profound impact on mental health and emotional well-being. Adolescence is a time of heightened vulnerability to mental health issues, such as depression, anxiety, and eating disorders. Research has consistently shown that low self-esteem is a significant risk factor for the development of these mental health issues in teenagers. When adolescents have low self-esteem, they are more likely to experience feelings of inadequacy, worthlessness, and self-doubt, which can contribute to the onset of mental health problems. On the other hand, teenagers with high self-esteem are more resilient in the face of life's challenges, have a more positive outlook on life, and are better equipped to cope with stress and adversity. By nurturing positive self-esteem in teenagers, parents, educators, and mental health professionals can help protect them from the negative impact of mental health issues and promote their overall well-being.

In addition to its influence on mental health, self-esteem also plays a critical role in shaping teenagers' social development and relationships. Adolescence is a time of intense socialization, as teenagers seek to establish their identity and place within peer groups and social networks. Healthy self-esteem provides adolescents with a sense of confidence, self-assurance, and self-respect that can help them navigate the complexities of social interactions, peer pressure, and conflicts with peers. It also enables teenagers to form secure and stable relationships with others, based on mutual respect, trust, and positive communication. Research has shown that teenagers with high self-esteem are more likely to have positive peer relationships, engage in healthy social behaviors, and experience greater social support and acceptance from others. By fostering positive self-esteem in teenagers, parents, educators, and community members can help them develop the social skills and resilience needed to navigate the challenges of adolescence and build meaningful and fulfilling relationships with others.

Furthermore, self-esteem is a critical factor in shaping teenagers' academic performance and achievement. Adolescence is a time of increased academic demands and pressure, as teenagers strive to excel in school, meet expectations from parents and educators, and prepare for future academic and career goals. Research has shown that self-esteem has a significant impact on students' motivation, engagement, and achievement in school. Teenagers with high self-esteem are more likely to set ambitious goals, work diligently towards their academic objectives, and persist in the face of difficulties and setbacks. They are also more likely to participate actively in classroom activities, seek out challenging opportunities for learning and growth, and take ownership of their academic success. In contrast, teenagers with low self-esteem may struggle to engage with schoolwork, lack confidence in their abilities, and experience feelings of helplessness and inadequacy that hinder their academic performance. By nurturing positive self-esteem in teenagers, parents, educators, and school counselors can support their academic success and promote a lifelong love of learning and achievement. During the critical period of adolescence, it is essential for teenagers to develop a healthy level of self-esteem to navigate the challenges of identity formation, socialization, and academic achievement. By fostering positive self-esteem in teenagers, parents, educators, and mental health professionals can help protect them from the negative impact of mental health issues, promote their social development and relationships, and support their academic success and achievement. Through positive reinforcement, encouragement, and support, adults can contribute to the healthy development of teenagers' self-esteem and empower them to thrive during this formative period of growth and self-discovery.

- Building self-confidence in teenagers

Building self-confidence in teenagers is a crucial aspect of their development and growth. Self-confidence is the belief in one's abilities and the recognition of one's worth and value. It plays a significant role in shaping teenagers' overall well-being, resilience, and success in various aspects of their lives, including academics, relationships, and future career endeavors. Teenagers who possess high levels of self-confidence are more likely to take on challenges, set ambitious goals, and persevere in the face of obstacles. They are also more likely to have positive self-esteem, self-worth, and a strong sense of identity.

There are several strategies that can help teenagers build and enhance their self-confidence. One of the most important factors is to create a supportive and nurturing environment in which teenagers feel valued, respected, and encouraged to express themselves. Parents, teachers, and mentors play a crucial role in shaping teenagers' self-confidence by providing positive feedback, constructive criticism, and emotional support. It is essential to listen to teenagers' thoughts, feelings, and concerns, and to validate their experiences and perspectives.

Another key aspect of building self-confidence in teenagers is to help them develop a growth mindset. A growth mindset is the belief that intelligence, talents, and abilities can be developed and improved through effort, perseverance, and learning from mistakes. Teenagers with a growth mindset are more likely to view challenges as opportunities for growth and learning, rather than as threats to their self-esteem. Encouraging teenagers to adopt a growth mindset can help them overcome self-doubt, fear of failure, and perfectionism, and cultivate a sense of resilience, optimism, and self-efficacy.

Moreover, setting realistic and achievable goals is an effective way to build teenagers' self-confidence. By setting specific, measurable, attainable, relevant, and time-bound (SMART) goals, teenagers can focus their efforts and energy on taking small steps towards their desired outcomes. Achieving these goals can help teenagers build a sense of competence, mastery, and accomplishment, which can boost their self-confidence and motivation. It is important to celebrate and recognize teenagers' progress and successes along the way, and to provide them with positive reinforcement and encouragement.

Additionally, engaging teenagers in activities and experiences that challenge them, build their skills and competencies, and foster their interests and passions can help boost their self-confidence. Participation in extracurricular activities, sports, hobbies, volunteer work, creative endeavors, and leadership roles can provide teenagers with opportunities to explore their talents, strengths, and capabilities, build positive relationships, and develop a sense of purpose and meaning. These activities can also help teenagers build resilience, problem-solving skills, emotional intelligence, and social skills, which are essential for building self-confidence.

Furthermore, fostering positive self-talk and self-compassion is essential for building teenagers' self-confidence. Helping teenagers develop a kind, supportive, and empowering internal dialogue can help them challenge negative beliefs, self-criticism, and self-doubt, and cultivate a sense of self-acceptance, self-love, and self-worth. Encouraging teenagers to practice mindfulness, relaxation techniques, and positive affirmations can help them manage stress, anxiety, and negative emotions, and cultivate a sense of inner peace, balance, and well-being. It is important to teach teenagers to be resilient, adaptable, and emotionally intelligent, and to help them develop healthy coping strategies for dealing with setbacks, challenges, and disappointments. By creating a supportive and nurturing environment, fostering a growth mindset, setting realistic goals, engaging in challenging activities, fostering positive self-talk, and practicing self-compassion, teenagers can develop a strong sense of self-confidence that will serve them well throughout their lives. As adults, it is our responsibility to help teenagers cultivate self-confidence, resilience, courage, and strength, and to empower them to pursue their dreams, achieve their goals, and realize their full potential. By investing in teenagers' self-confidence, we can help them become confident, capable, and empowered individuals who can contribute positively to society and make a difference in the world.

- Encouraging a positive self-image

Encouraging a positive self-image is an essential aspect of mental health and overall well-being. Self-image refers to the way individuals perceive themselves and their abilities, both physically and psychologically. It is influenced by various factors such as societal standards, personal experiences, and feedback from others. A positive self-image is linked to higher self-esteem, increased confidence, and better mental health outcomes. It is important to recognize that self-image is not fixed and can be influenced and shaped over time through self-reflection, positive affirmations, and self-care practices.

One key way to encourage a positive self-image is through self-reflection and self-awareness. Taking the time to reflect on one's thoughts, feelings, and actions can help individuals gain a better understanding of themselves and their strengths. This can involve reflecting on past experiences, identifying negative thought patterns, and challenging self-critical beliefs. By becoming more self-aware, individuals can begin to shift their focus from perceived flaws to their unique qualities and strengths, leading to a more positive self-image.

Another important way to foster a positive self-image is through positive affirmations and self-talk. Positive affirmations involve consciously choosing to focus on and repeat positive statements about oneself. This can help to counteract negative self-talk and self-doubt, promoting a more positive self-image. For example, individuals can practice affirmations such as "I am worthy," "I am capable," and "I deserve love and respect. " By incorporating positive affirmations into daily routines, individuals can gradually shift their mindset towards a more positive self-image.

Additionally, engaging in self-care practices can help to boost self-esteem and promote a positive self-image. Self-care involves taking time to prioritize one's physical, emotional, and mental well-being. This can include activities such as exercise, proper nutrition, adequate sleep, and relaxation techniques. By taking care of oneself, individuals can feel more confident, energized, and positive about themselves. Engaging in self-care practices can also serve as a form of self-love and self-compassion, reinforcing a positive self-image.

It is also important to surround oneself with supportive and positive relationships in order to encourage a positive self-image. The feedback and validation from others can play a significant role in how individuals perceive themselves. By building healthy relationships with individuals who uplift and support them, individuals can feel more valued and accepted, leading to a more positive self-image. Surrounding oneself with positive influences can help to counteract negative messages from society or past experiences, fostering a more positive self-image. By engaging in self-reflection, positive affirmations, self-care practices, and cultivating supportive relationships, individuals can begin to shift their mindset towards a more positive self-image. It is important to recognize that self-image is not fixed and can be influenced and shaped over time through intentional effort and self-care. By prioritizing self-love, self-compassion, and self-acceptance, individuals can cultivate a positive self-image that reflects their unique qualities and strengths.

Chapter 6: Addressing Behavioral Challenges

- IDENTIFYING PROBLEMATIC behaviors in teens

During adolescence, many teens experience a range of emotions and behaviors as they navigate the complex transition into adulthood. While some level of moodiness and rebellion is considered normal during this stage of development, there are certain behaviors that may signal underlying problems that require intervention. Identifying problematic behaviors in teens is essential in order to address issues early on and prevent them from escalating into more serious problems.

One of the key indicators of problematic behavior in teens is sudden changes in mood or behavior. This can manifest as extreme irritability, aggression, withdrawal, or mood swings that are significantly different from the teen's usual demeanor. These changes may be a sign of underlying mental health issues such as depression, anxiety, or substance abuse. It is important for parents and caregivers to pay attention to these changes and seek professional help if they persist over an extended period of time.

Another red flag to watch out for is academic problems or a decline in school performance. While some level of academic struggle is normal for teens, consistent poor grades, skipping classes, or frequent disciplinary issues at school may be indicative of larger issues at play. These behaviors could be a sign of underlying learning disabilities, attention deficits, or emotional distress that may require intervention from teachers, counselors, or mental health professionals.

Substance abuse is another common problematic behavior that many teens may engage in. Experimenting with drugs or alcohol is unfortunately a common rite of passage for many adolescents, but if these behaviors become more frequent or escalate to the point of dependence, it is a cause for concern.

Substance abuse can have serious physical, emotional, and legal consequences for teens, and it is important for parents to address these behaviors early on and seek help from addiction specialists or counselors.

Another problematic behavior in teens to watch out for is risky or dangerous activities. This can include reckless driving, unprotected sex, or engaging in criminal behavior. These actions can put teens at risk for serious injury, illness, or legal consequences, and it is crucial for parents to set clear boundaries and consequences for risky behaviors. It is also important to encourage open communication with teens about the potential consequences of their actions and to provide them with guidance and support in making safer choices.

Lastly, changes in social relationships can also signal problematic behaviors in teens. This can include sudden changes in peer groups, isolation from friends and family, or conflicts with authority figures. Teens may also exhibit manipulative or deceitful behaviors in their relationships, which can be a sign of underlying issues such as low self-esteem or a need for attention. It is important for parents to monitor their teen's social interactions and provide guidance and support in navigating healthy relationships. By paying attention to changes in mood or behavior, academic problems, substance abuse, risky activities, and social relationships, parents and caregivers can provide the necessary support and intervention to help teens navigate the challenges of adolescence. It is important to approach these issues with understanding and compassion, while also setting clear boundaries and seeking professional help when needed. By addressing problematic behaviors early on, we can help teens build resilience, coping skills, and healthy relationships that will serve them well throughout their lives.

- Strategies for addressing and managing behavioral issues

Behavioral issues can arise in various settings, including schools, workplaces, and even within families. These issues can negatively impact relationships, productivity, and overall well-being if left unaddressed. Therefore, it is important to have effective strategies in place for addressing and managing behavioral issues when they arise. In this article, we will discuss some key strategies that can help individuals and organizations effectively address and manage behavioral issues.

One important strategy for addressing behavioral issues is to create a positive and supportive environment. Research has shown that individuals are more likely to exhibit positive behaviors when they feel supported and valued. By creating a positive environment, individuals are more likely to feel motivated to change their behaviors in a positive way. One way to create a positive environment is to provide positive reinforcement for desired behaviors. This can be done through praise, rewards, or other forms of recognition. By providing positive reinforcement, individuals are more likely to continue exhibiting positive behaviors.

Another important strategy for addressing behavioral issues is to set clear expectations and consequences. Clear expectations help individuals understand what is expected of them and what behaviors are acceptable. By setting clear expectations, individuals are more likely to understand the consequences of their actions and make informed decisions about their behavior. Additionally, clear consequences help individuals understand the potential outcomes of their actions and can motivate them to make positive choices. By setting clear expectations and consequences, individuals are more likely to exhibit positive behaviors and make positive changes.

It is also important to provide individuals with the support and resources they need to address their behavioral issues. This can include providing access to counseling, therapy, or other forms of support. By providing individuals with the support they need, they are more likely to address their behavioral issues in a healthy and productive way. Additionally, providing resources such as educational materials or workshops can help individuals learn more about their behavioral issues and how to manage them effectively. By providing support and resources, individuals are more likely to make positive changes and improve their behavior.

Effective communication is another key strategy for addressing behavioral issues. Clear and open communication can help individuals understand their behaviors, identify areas for improvement, and work towards positive changes. By communicating openly and honestly, individuals are more likely to feel heard and valued, which can motivate them to address their behavioral issues. Additionally, effective communication can help individuals understand the impact of their behaviors on others and on the overall environment. By promoting open communication, individuals can work together to address behavioral issues in a proactive and collaborative way. By implementing these strategies, individuals and organizations can effectively address behavioral issues and promote positive changes in behavior. It is important to approach behavioral issues with empathy, understanding, and a willingness to work together towards solutions. By taking a proactive and collaborative approach, individuals and organizations can create a supportive and positive environment that promotes healthy behaviors and overall well-being.

- Seeking professional help when needed

Seeking professional help when needed is a critical step in maintaining emotional and mental well-being. In today's fast-paced and demanding world, many individuals may find themselves struggling with various challenges, such as anxiety, depression, relationship issues, or other mental health concerns. It is important to recognize that asking for help is not a sign of weakness, but rather a courageous and proactive step towards addressing and resolving these challenges.

One of the most common barriers to seeking professional help is stigma surrounding mental health issues. Society has unfortunately perpetuated the idea that seeking help for mental health concerns is something to be ashamed of or looked down upon. This stigma can often prevent individuals from reaching out to a therapist, counselor, or psychologist for assistance. It is crucial to challenge and dismantle these harmful beliefs, as seeking professional help is a sign of strength and self-awareness, not weakness or failure.

Another barrier to seeking professional help is a lack of awareness or understanding about mental health resources and services available. Many individuals may not be aware of the various mental health professionals, therapy modalities, or treatment options that are accessible to them. It is essential to educate oneself about the different types of mental health professionals, such as therapists, counselors, psychologists, and psychiatrists, and the services they provide. By having a better understanding of the available resources, individuals can make more informed decisions about seeking professional help.

Additionally, fear of judgment or confidentiality breaches may prevent individuals from seeking professional help. Many individuals may worry about what others will think if they seek therapy or counseling, or fear that their personal information will not be kept confidential by mental health professionals. It is important to remember that mental health professionals are bound by ethical guidelines and legal standards to maintain confidentiality and protect the privacy of their clients. Seeking professional help is a private and confidential process that should be respected and upheld by mental health professionals.

Furthermore, financial concerns can also be a significant barrier to seeking professional help. Many individuals may worry about the cost of therapy or counseling sessions, especially if they do not have health insurance coverage for mental health services. It is important to explore and inquire about affordable mental health resources and services, such as community mental health centers, sliding scale fees, or online therapy platforms. Some employers also offer employee assistance programs (EAPs) that provide free or discounted mental health services to their employees. It is essential to prioritize mental health and well-being, and not let financial concerns deter one from seeking professional help when needed. Whether struggling with anxiety, depression, relationship issues, or other mental health concerns, it is important to recognize the importance of reaching out to a therapist, counselor, or psychologist for assistance. By challenging stigma, increasing awareness, overcoming fears, and addressing financial concerns, individuals can break down barriers to seeking professional help and prioritize their mental health and well-being. Remember, asking for help is a sign of strength and courage, not weakness or failure.

Chapter 7: Supporting Mental Health

- ## RECOGNIZING THE SIGNS of mental health issues in teens

It is essential for parents, teachers, and other adults to be able to recognize the signs of mental health issues in teenagers in order to provide timely support and intervention. Adolescence is a period of rapid physical, emotional, and social development, and many teens may experience challenges and stressors that can impact their mental well-being. By being able to identify early warning signs, adults can help teens access the resources and treatment they need to overcome mental health issues and thrive.

One common sign of mental health issues in teens is changes in behavior. This can include withdrawal from friends and family, sudden mood swings, irritability, or aggression. Teens may also exhibit changes in sleeping or eating patterns, such as trouble falling asleep or excessive sleeping, or significant changes in appetite. These behavioral changes can be indicative of underlying mental health issues, such as depression, anxiety, or substance abuse.

Another important sign of mental health issues in teens is changes in academic performance. Teens who are struggling with mental health issues may experience difficulty concentrating, have trouble completing assignments, or exhibit a sudden decline in grades. They may also skip school or avoid social activities that they once enjoyed. It is important for adults to pay attention to these changes and offer support and resources to help teens cope with their mental health challenges.

Physical symptoms can also be a sign of underlying mental health issues in teens. These can include headaches, stomachaches, or other unexplained physical complaints. While these symptoms may have a medical explanation, they can also be a manifestation of stress, anxiety, or other mental health issues.

It is important for adults to take these physical symptoms seriously and help teens access appropriate care and treatment.

Teens who are experiencing mental health issues may also exhibit changes in their interpersonal relationships. They may become more isolated, avoid social interactions, or have difficulty forming and maintaining friendships. Teens may also exhibit changes in their romantic relationships, such as increased conflict or avoidance of their partner. By paying attention to these changes in interpersonal relationships, adults can provide support and guidance to help teens navigate their mental health challenges.

It is important for adults to be aware of the signs of mental health issues in teens and to take them seriously. Early intervention is key to helping teens overcome mental health challenges and prevent more serious consequences in the future. By recognizing the signs of mental health issues in teens and offering support and resources, adults can help teens build resilience, coping skills, and overall well-being. By paying attention to changes in behavior, academic performance, physical symptoms, and interpersonal relationships, adults can identify early warning signs of mental health issues and intervene appropriately. With timely support and intervention, teens can overcome mental health challenges and thrive in their academic, social, and personal lives.

- Providing emotional support and guidance

Emotional support and guidance are essential components of mental health and well-being. As human beings, we all experience a wide range of emotions, from joy and excitement to sadness and anxiety. During difficult times, having the support of others can make a world of difference. Whether it's going through a breakup, dealing with a loss, or facing a challenging situation at work, having someone to lean on can lighten the burden and provide comfort.

One of the key aspects of providing emotional support and guidance is active listening. This means being fully present and engaged in the conversation, giving the person your undivided attention. It involves not just hearing what they are saying, but truly understanding their emotions and perspective. Active listening also means asking open-ended questions to encourage them to express themselves more fully and openly. By demonstrating empathy and genuine interest in their well-being, you create a safe space for them to share their thoughts and feelings.

Another important aspect of providing emotional support is validation. It's essential to acknowledge and validate the person's emotions, even if you may not fully understand or agree with them. Validation helps the person feel heard and understood, which can be incredibly comforting during challenging times. It's important to remember that everyone experiences emotions differently, and what may seem trivial to one person can be deeply distressing to another. By validating their feelings, you show compassion and respect for their emotional experience.

In addition to active listening and validation, providing emotional support and guidance also involves offering practical help and solutions. Sometimes, all a person needs is a listening ear and a shoulder to lean on. Other times, they may benefit from practical advice or resources to help them navigate their emotions and challenges. As a supportive figure, it's important to assess the person's needs and offer appropriate help without being pushy or overbearing. You can help them brainstorm potential solutions, connect them with relevant support services, or simply offer a fresh perspective on their situation.

Furthermore, building trust and rapport is essential in providing effective emotional support and guidance. Trust is the foundation of any meaningful relationship, and it's particularly important in a support role. By demonstrating reliability, empathy, and confidentiality, you can earn the person's trust and create a strong bond of connection. Trusting relationships provide a safe space for vulnerability and open communication, allowing the person to share their deepest fears and insecurities without fear of judgment or betrayal. Building trust takes time and effort, but it's a crucial aspect of providing effective emotional support.

It's also important to set boundaries and practice self-care when providing emotional support and guidance. While it's crucial to be a supportive figure, it's equally important to take care of your own mental and emotional well-being. Providing support can be emotionally draining, especially if you're dealing with your own challenges. Setting boundaries helps you maintain a healthy balance and avoid burnout. It's okay to take breaks, prioritize your own needs, and seek support from others when necessary. Remember, you can't pour from an empty cup, so it's essential to prioritize your own well-being while supporting others. By actively listening, validating emotions, offering practical help, building trust, and setting boundaries, you can offer meaningful support to those in need.

Remember that everyone experiences emotions differently, and it's crucial to approach each situation with empathy, compassion, and respect. By creating a safe space for open communication and vulnerability, you can make a positive impact on the lives of those around you. So, don't hesitate to reach out a helping hand and provide the emotional support and guidance that others may need.

- Accessing resources for mental health support

Accessing resources for mental health support is an essential step in maintaining your overall well-being and mental health. In today's fast-paced and stressful world, it is common to experience feelings of anxiety, depression, or other mental health challenges. Seeking help and support is not a sign of weakness, but rather a sign of strength and self-awareness. There are a variety of resources available to support individuals in their mental health journey, including therapy, counseling, support groups, hotlines, and online resources.

Therapy is one of the most common forms of mental health support and can be highly beneficial for individuals struggling with a range of mental health issues. Therapy provides a safe and confidential space for individuals to explore their thoughts and feelings, gain insight into their behaviors and patterns, and develop coping strategies for managing stress and anxiety. There are many different types of therapy available, including cognitive-behavioral therapy, psychotherapy, and dialectical behavior therapy, among others. It is important to find a therapist who is experienced in treating your specific concerns and who you feel comfortable working with.

In addition to therapy, counseling can be a helpful resource for individuals seeking support for their mental health. Counseling typically focuses on providing practical advice, guidance, and support to help individuals navigate their mental health challenges. Counselors can help individuals identify triggers for their symptoms, develop coping strategies, and set goals for improving their mental health. Counseling can be particularly beneficial for individuals who are looking for short-term support or guidance in managing specific issues or concerns.

Support groups are another valuable resource for individuals seeking mental health support. Support groups can provide a sense of community and belonging, as well as the opportunity to connect with others who are facing similar challenges. Support groups can be especially helpful for individuals dealing with specific issues, such as addiction, grief, or trauma. By sharing their experiences and learning from others, individuals can gain valuable insights, encouragement, and support in their mental health journey.

Hotlines are another important resource for individuals in need of immediate mental health support. There are a variety of hotlines available that provide confidential and anonymous support for individuals in crisis or experiencing emotional distress. Hotlines are staffed by trained professionals who can provide crisis intervention, emotional support, and referrals to additional resources. Hotlines can be particularly helpful for individuals who are feeling overwhelmed, hopeless, or in need of immediate assistance.

Online resources have become increasingly popular for individuals seeking mental health support. There are a wide range of online resources available, including websites, forums, chat rooms, and apps, that can provide information, support, and tools for managing mental health concerns. Online resources can be especially helpful for individuals who may not have access to traditional mental health services, such as those living in remote areas or with limited financial resources. Online resources can also be a convenient and flexible option for individuals who prefer to seek support from the comfort of their own home. There are a variety of resources available to support individuals in their mental health journey, including therapy, counseling, support groups, hotlines, and online resources. By reaching out for help and support, individuals can gain valuable insights, coping strategies, and connections to others who understand their struggles. Remember, seeking help is a sign of strength and self-awareness, and there is no shame in reaching out for support when you need it.

Chapter 8: Navigating Peer Pressure

- UNDERSTANDING THE influence of peers on teen behavior

Peer influence is a powerful force on teen behavior, shaping their attitudes, beliefs, and actions in significant ways. Adolescents are uniquely susceptible to the influence of their peers due to their developmental stage and the importance they place on social relationships. As teens navigate the complex landscape of adolescence, they often turn to their peers for guidance, validation, and support. This can result in both positive and negative outcomes, as friends can either encourage healthy behaviors or lead teens down risky paths.

It is important to understand how peer influence operates in order to support adolescents in making informed choices and promoting positive behavior. Research has shown that peers play a crucial role in shaping teen behavior in various aspects of their lives, including academics, relationships, and health. For example, studies have demonstrated that teens who have friends who value academic success are more likely to perform well in school themselves. On the other hand, adolescents who associate with peers who engage in risky behaviors, such as substance abuse or delinquency, are more likely to adopt these behaviors themselves.

One of the key factors influencing peer influence on teen behavior is the concept of social norms. Social norms are unwritten rules that dictate how individuals should behave in a given social context. When teens are surrounded by peers who adhere to certain norms, they are more likely to conform to these norms themselves. This conformity can lead to positive outcomes, such as encouraging healthy habits or academic achievement, but it can also result in negative behaviors if the social norms are harmful or risky.

Another important aspect of peer influence on teen behavior is the concept of social comparison. Adolescents often compare themselves to their peers in terms of appearance, intelligence, popularity, and other attributes. This comparison can lead to feelings of inadequacy or pressure to conform to certain standards set by their peers. In some cases, teens may engage in behaviors they wouldn't normally engage in just to fit in or gain acceptance from their peers.

Peer influence can also be mediated by individual factors, such as personality traits and self-esteem. Teens who have high levels of self-esteem and strong personal values may be less susceptible to the influence of their peers, as they are more confident in their own beliefs and choices. Conversely, teens who have low self-esteem or lack a sense of identity may be more likely to adopt the behaviors of their peers in order to feel accepted and validated. Understanding the mechanisms through which peers influence adolescents can help parents, educators, and other stakeholders support teens in making positive choices and avoiding risky behaviors. By fostering positive peer relationships, promoting healthy social norms, and empowering teens to develop strong self-esteem and personal values, we can help mitigate the negative impact of peer influence on teen behavior and promote positive outcomes for adolescents.

- Strategies for helping teens resist negative peer pressure

Peer pressure is a common phenomenon that many teenagers face on a daily basis. It can manifest in various forms, such as pressure to try drugs or alcohol, engage in risky behaviors, or conform to certain social norms. Negative peer pressure can have detrimental effects on a teenager's well-being and can lead to serious consequences if not addressed properly. In order to help teenagers resist negative peer pressure, it is important for parents, educators, and other adults in their lives to implement strategies that empower them to make informed and independent decisions.

One of the most important strategies for helping teens resist negative peer pressure is to foster open and honest communication. Establishing a strong foundation of trust and understanding between teens and their parents or caregivers can create a supportive environment where teenagers feel comfortable discussing their concerns and seeking guidance. By encouraging teens to voice their opinions and express their values, adults can help them develop a sense of self-assurance and assertiveness when faced with peer pressure. Additionally, adults should actively listen to teens and validate their feelings, which can help strengthen their emotional resilience and confidence in standing up to negative influences.

Another effective strategy for helping teens resist negative peer pressure is to educate them about the potential consequences of succumbing to peer pressure. Providing teens with accurate information about the risks and dangers associated with certain behaviors, such as drug and alcohol use, can help them make informed decisions and understand the importance of staying true to their values. Adults can also engage teens in discussions about the role of peer pressure in shaping behavior and encourage critical thinking skills that enable them to evaluate the motives of their peers and the potential impact of their actions.

In addition to communication and education, it is essential to empower teens with the tools and resources they need to resist negative peer pressure. This can include teaching them effective refusal skills, such as confidently saying "no" to peer pressure and offering alternative solutions or compromises. Role-playing scenarios in which teens practice refusing negative influences can help them feel more prepared and confident when faced with real-life situations. Adults can also encourage teens to surround themselves with positive influences and supportive friends who share similar values and goals, which can help reduce the likelihood of succumbing to negative peer pressure.

Furthermore, adults can help teens build their self-esteem and self-confidence by recognizing and affirming their strengths and accomplishments. By highlighting their unique qualities and talents, adults can instill a sense of pride and self-worth in teens, which can provide them with the resilience and self-assurance needed to resist negative peer pressure. Encouraging teens to participate in positive activities and pursue their interests can also help them build a strong sense of identity and purpose, making them less susceptible to the influence of peers who may engage in risky or harmful behaviors. By fostering a trusting and understanding relationship with teens, adults can create a safe and supportive environment where teenagers feel comfortable discussing their concerns and seeking guidance. Educating teens about the potential consequences of succumbing to peer pressure and empowering them with the skills and resources they need to resist negative influences can help them make informed decisions and stay true to their values. Ultimately, by equipping teens with the tools and support they need to navigate peer pressure, adults can help them build resilience, confidence, and self-assurance in facing challenges and making positive choices.

- Promoting healthy friendships and relationships

Friendships and relationships play a crucial role in our overall well-being and mental health. Healthy friendships can bring joy, support, and a sense of belonging to our lives, while toxic relationships can have negative impacts on our mental and physical health. Therefore, promoting healthy friendships and relationships is essential for maintaining a happy and fulfilling life.

One key aspect of promoting healthy friendships and relationships is setting boundaries. Boundaries are essential in any relationship, as they help define what is acceptable and what is not. By setting boundaries, we communicate our needs and values to others, which can help prevent misunderstandings and conflicts. It is important to communicate these boundaries clearly and assertively, while also respecting the boundaries of others. This can help foster mutual respect and trust in our relationships.

Another important aspect of promoting healthy friendships and relationships is practicing good communication skills. Effective communication is key to building strong and meaningful relationships. By actively listening to others, expressing our thoughts and feelings clearly, and being empathetic and supportive, we can create a safe and nurturing environment for our relationships to thrive. Healthy communication can also help resolve conflicts and misunderstandings in a constructive and respectful manner.

Furthermore, promoting healthy friendships and relationships involves cultivating mutual trust and respect. Trust is the foundation of any healthy relationship, as it allows us to feel secure and valued in our connections with others. Building trust takes time and effort, but it is essential for creating a strong and resilient bond with friends and loved ones. Respect is also crucial in maintaining healthy relationships, as it shows that we value and appreciate the feelings and boundaries of others. By treating each other with respect and honoring each other's autonomy, we can create a harmonious and fulfilling relationship.

In addition, promoting healthy friendships and relationships involves fostering a sense of mutual support and positivity. Friends and loved ones are often our sources of comfort and encouragement during challenging times. By being there for each other, offering a listening ear, and providing emotional support, we can strengthen our relationships and deepen our connections with others. It is also important to celebrate the successes and accomplishments of our friends and loved ones, as this can help boost their self-esteem and promote a positive and uplifting atmosphere in our relationships.

Furthermore, promoting healthy friendships and relationships involves being mindful of the quality of our interactions with others. It is important to surround ourselves with people who uplift and inspire us, rather than bring us down or drain our energy. By being selective about the company we keep and nurturing relationships that are positive and fulfilling, we can create a supportive and nurturing social circle that enhances our well-being and happiness. This also includes being aware of red flags in relationships, such as controlling behavior, manipulation, or disrespect, and taking steps to address these issues in a healthy and constructive manner. By setting boundaries, practicing good communication skills, cultivating trust and respect, fostering mutual support and positivity, and being mindful of the quality of our interactions, we can build strong and meaningful connections with others that contribute to our overall well-being and mental health. Ultimately, healthy friendships and relationships are a source of joy, support, and connection that enrich our lives and help us navigate the challenges and joys of the human experience.

Chapter 9: Encouraging Independence and Responsibility

- ## BALANCING INDEPENDENCE and guidance for teens

As adolescents navigate the transition from childhood to adulthood, they are faced with the challenge of balancing independence and guidance. This delicate balance is essential for their development and growth, as it allows them to explore their own identities and make informed decisions while still receiving support and structure from trusted adults. Teenagers crave independence as they seek to assert their autonomy and establish their own sense of self. However, they also need guidance and support from adults to help them navigate the complexities of adolescence and make responsible choices.

One of the key factors in achieving a healthy balance between independence and guidance for teens is fostering open communication and mutual trust between parents or caregivers and adolescents. By establishing a foundation of trust and respect, teens are more likely to seek guidance and advice from adults when needed. It is important for adults to listen actively to teens, validate their feelings, and offer support without judgment. This open communication can help teens feel empowered to make their own decisions while still seeking guidance from trusted adults.

Another important aspect of balancing independence and guidance for teens is setting clear boundaries and expectations. While teenagers may want to assert their independence, they still need structure and boundaries to help them make responsible choices. Adults can help teens navigate this balance by setting clear rules and consequences, while also allowing space for them to make their own decisions and learn from their mistakes. By establishing clear boundaries and expectations, adults can provide guidance and support while still allowing teens the freedom to explore their own identities.

It is also crucial for adults to provide teens with opportunities for independence and decision-making. Allowing teens to have a say in their own lives and giving them opportunities to make choices can help them develop important skills such as critical thinking, problem-solving, and self-regulation. Adults can support teens in this process by offering guidance and feedback, but ultimately allowing them to make their own decisions and learn from the consequences. By providing teens with opportunities for independence, adults can help them develop the confidence and skills they need to navigate the challenges of adolescence and become responsible, independent adults.

In addition to fostering communication, setting boundaries, and providing opportunities for independence, it is important for adults to model healthy behaviors and attitudes for teens. Adolescents learn by observing the behavior of the adults in their lives, and it is essential for adults to model positive and respectful communication, decision-making, and problem-solving skills. By modeling healthy behaviors and attitudes, adults can help teens develop the skills and values they need to navigate the complexities of adolescence and make informed choices. Adults can also provide guidance and support by sharing their own experiences and knowledge, offering advice, and being a supportive presence in teens' lives. By fostering a trusting and supportive relationship with teens, adults can help them navigate the challenges of adolescence and develop the skills and values they need to become responsible, independent adults. With the right support and guidance, teenagers can successfully navigate the transition from childhood to adulthood and grow into confident, capable individuals.

- Fostering a sense of responsibility in teenagers

Fostering a sense of responsibility in teenagers is a crucial aspect of their development and growth into capable, independent adults. Responsibility is the ability to take ownership of one's actions, decisions, and obligations. It involves being accountable for the consequences of those actions and making thoughtful and ethical choices. Instilling a sense of responsibility in teenagers helps them navigate the challenges and complexities of the world with maturity and integrity.

One of the key ways to foster a sense of responsibility in teenagers is to provide them with opportunities to make decisions and take on tasks that require them to be accountable for their actions. This can be done through assigning them tasks and responsibilities in the home, school, or community, such as chores, school projects, or volunteering. By giving teenagers the opportunity to take on these responsibilities, they learn the importance of following through on commitments, meeting deadlines, and prioritizing tasks.

Another important way to foster a sense of responsibility in teenagers is to model responsible behavior yourself. As adults, we serve as role models for the teenagers in our lives, and they often look to us for guidance on how to navigate the challenges of growing up. By demonstrating responsible behavior, such as fulfilling our own commitments, keeping our word, and making ethical decisions, we show teenagers what it means to be responsible and set a positive example for them to follow.

In addition to modeling responsible behavior, it is important to provide teenagers with guidance and support as they navigate the complexities of growing up. This can involve having open and honest conversations with them about the importance of responsibility, the consequences of their actions, and the value of making ethical choices. By engaging in these conversations and offering guidance and support, teenagers can develop a better understanding of what it means to be responsible and the importance of taking ownership of their actions.

It is also important to create a supportive and nurturing environment for teenagers to cultivate a sense of responsibility. This can involve providing them with encouragement and praise when they demonstrate responsible behavior, as well as offering constructive feedback and guidance when they make mistakes. By creating a safe and supportive environment for teenagers to learn and grow, they are more likely to feel empowered to take on new responsibilities and make ethical choices.

Furthermore, it is important to involve teenagers in decision-making processes and encourage them to contribute their opinions and ideas. By involving teenagers in decision-making processes, they feel a sense of ownership and responsibility for the outcomes of those decisions. This can help them develop critical thinking skills, problem-solving abilities, and a sense of agency in their own lives. By empowering teenagers to be active participants in decision-making processes, they are more likely to take responsibility for their choices and actions. By providing them with opportunities to make decisions and take on responsibilities, modeling responsible behavior, offering guidance and support, creating a supportive environment, and involving them in decision-making processes, we can help teenagers cultivate a strong sense of responsibility that will serve them well throughout their lives. Ultimately, by instilling a sense of responsibility in teenagers, we empower them to navigate the challenges of the world with maturity, integrity, and a strong sense of self.

- Encouraging autonomy and decision-making skills

Autonomy and decision-making skills are essential components of personal development and success in both professional and personal spheres. Encouraging autonomy and decision-making skills in individuals is crucial for fostering independence, confidence, and accountability. By empowering individuals to make their own choices and take responsibility for their actions, they are better equipped to navigate the challenges and opportunities that come their way.

There are several strategies that can be employed to encourage autonomy and decision-making skills in individuals. Firstly, it is important to create a supportive and empowering environment where individuals feel safe to express themselves and take risks. This can be achieved by providing opportunities for open communication, feedback, and collaboration. By encouraging individuals to voice their opinions, share their ideas, and participate in decision-making processes, they are more likely to develop a sense of ownership and agency in their actions.

Another important strategy for promoting autonomy and decision-making skills is to provide individuals with the tools and resources they need to make informed choices. This includes providing access to information, training, and mentorship opportunities that can help individuals develop their critical thinking, problem-solving, and decision-making skills. By equipping individuals with the knowledge and skills they need to assess situations, weigh options, and make decisions, they are better prepared to take on challenges and seize opportunities.

Furthermore, it is important to foster a culture of trust and empowerment in which individuals feel valued, respected, and supported in their autonomy and decision-making processes. This can be achieved by delegating responsibilities, giving individuals the freedom to take risks, and providing opportunities for growth and development. By demonstrating confidence in individuals' abilities to make sound decisions and learn from their mistakes, they are more likely to take initiative, show resilience, and demonstrate accountability in their actions.

It is also important to recognize that autonomy and decision-making skills are not innate abilities but rather competencies that can be developed and refined over time. Therefore, it is important to provide individuals with ongoing opportunities for practice, reflection, and feedback in order to strengthen their autonomy and decision-making skills. This can be done through formal training programs, mentoring relationships, experiential learning opportunities, and other resources that can help individuals build their confidence, competence, and capacity to make informed decisions. By creating a supportive and empowering environment, providing individuals with the tools and resources they need, fostering a culture of trust and empowerment, and offering ongoing opportunities for practice and feedback, individuals can develop the autonomy and decision-making skills they need to navigate the complexities of the modern world. By promoting autonomy and decision-making skills, we can empower individuals to take control of their lives, seize opportunities, and achieve their full potential.

Chapter 10: Fostering Resilience in Teens

- BUILDING RESILIENCE in teens to cope with challenges

In today's fast-paced and ever-changing world, teenagers face a myriad of challenges and obstacles on a daily basis. From academic pressures to social media influence, navigating adolescence can be a daunting task for many young individuals. It is essential for teens to build resilience in order to cope with these challenges and emerge stronger and more confident in their abilities. Resilience is the ability to bounce back from difficult situations and setbacks, and it is a crucial skill that can help teenagers navigate the ups and downs of life with grace and perseverance.

One of the key components of building resilience in teens is fostering a sense of self-esteem and self-worth. Teenagers who have a strong sense of self-esteem are more likely to weather the storms of adolescence with confidence and resilience. Encouraging teens to develop a positive self-image and to recognize their own worth can go a long way in helping them cope with challenges and setbacks. Parents, teachers, and other important figures in a teenager's life play a crucial role in building and nurturing a teen's self-esteem, and it is important for these adults to provide positive reinforcement and support to help teens develop a healthy sense of self.

Another important aspect of building resilience in teens is teaching them how to manage stress and cope with difficult emotions. Adolescence can be a time of great emotional turmoil, as teens navigate the complexities of identity formation and social relationships. It is important for teens to learn healthy coping mechanisms for managing stress and emotions, such as practicing mindfulness, engaging in regular physical activity, and seeking support from trusted adults or peers. By teaching teens how to effectively cope with stress and emotions, we can empower them to navigate the challenges of adolescence with resilience and strength.

Building strong social connections is also crucial in helping teens develop resilience. Social support from friends, family, and other important figures in a teen's life can help them feel valued, understood, and supported during difficult times. Encouraging teens to cultivate positive social relationships and to seek out supportive individuals can help them build a strong network of social support that can bolster their resilience in the face of challenges. Additionally, engaging in activities and hobbies that promote social connection, such as team sports or community service, can help teens build resilience by fostering a sense of belonging and connection to others.

In addition to developing self-esteem, coping skills, and social connections, it is important for teens to cultivate a growth mindset in order to build resilience. A growth mindset is the belief that one's abilities and intelligence can be developed through effort and perseverance, rather than being fixed traits. Encouraging teens to adopt a growth mindset can help them approach challenges and setbacks with a sense of optimism and determination, knowing that they have the capacity to learn and grow from their experiences. By fostering a growth mindset in teens, we can help them develop the resilience needed to navigate the uncertainties and difficulties of adolescence with confidence and resilience. By empowering teens to develop these key skills and traits, we can help them navigate the challenges of adolescence with grace and strength. Through positive reinforcement, support, and encouragement, we can help teens build the resilience needed to overcome life's obstacles and emerge stronger and more confident in their abilities. By equipping teens with the tools and skills necessary to cope with challenges, we can help them thrive and flourish during this formative stage of development.

- Helping teens develop coping mechanisms

Adolescence is a period of great change and transition, both physically and emotionally. It is during this time that teens are faced with numerous challenges and stressors that can impact their mental health and well-being. Helping teens develop healthy coping mechanisms is essential in order to support their emotional resilience and empower them to navigate the various difficulties they may encounter.

One of the key aspects of helping teens develop coping mechanisms is to promote self-awareness and emotional intelligence. Teens need to understand and recognize their emotions in order to effectively manage them. By encouraging teens to identify and express their feelings, they can learn to cope with stress in a more constructive manner. This may involve teaching teens techniques such as journaling, mindfulness, or deep breathing exercises to help them regulate their emotions and reduce feelings of overwhelm.

Another important component of developing coping mechanisms in teens is providing them with a supportive and non-judgmental environment in which they can express themselves. This may involve creating open lines of communication where teens feel comfortable sharing their thoughts and feelings without fear of criticism or rejection. By fostering a sense of trust and understanding, teens can feel more empowered to seek help and support when needed.

In addition to promoting self-awareness and creating a supportive environment, it is also important to help teens build resilience and coping skills through practical strategies and tools. This may involve teaching teens problem-solving skills, time management techniques, and stress-reduction strategies that can help them navigate difficult situations more effectively. By equipping teens with these skills, they can develop a sense of control and agency in managing their emotions and coping with stress.

Furthermore, it is important to recognize that coping mechanisms are not a one-size-fits-all solution. Different teens may respond to stress and challenges in different ways, so it is important to provide a range of coping strategies and options for teens to explore. By encouraging teens to experiment with different techniques and find what works best for them, they can develop a personalized toolkit of coping mechanisms that they can use to navigate the ups and downs of adolescence.

It is also important to recognize the role of social support in helping teens develop coping mechanisms. Friends, family members, teachers, and other trusted adults can play a critical role in providing emotional support and guidance to teens during difficult times. By fostering strong relationships and networks of support, teens can feel more connected and less isolated, which can help them build resilience and cope with stress more effectively. By promoting self-awareness, creating a supportive environment, teaching practical coping skills, and encouraging social support, we can empower teens to navigate the ups and downs of adolescence with confidence and resilience. By investing in the emotional health and well-being of teens, we can help them build a strong foundation for lifelong mental health and well-being.

- Promoting mental and emotional well-being

Mental health refers to our emotional, psychological, and social well-being, while emotional well-being refers to our ability to cope with stress, regulate our emotions, and build healthy relationships. Both are interconnected and play a significant role in our daily lives.

There are various strategies and practices that can help promote mental and emotional well-being. One of the most important factors is self-care. This includes taking care of your physical health by eating well, exercising regularly, getting enough sleep, and avoiding harmful substances such as drugs and alcohol. It also involves taking care of your emotional health by practicing self-compassion, setting boundaries, and seeking support when needed.

Another important aspect of promoting mental and emotional well-being is building strong relationships. Having a support system of friends and family members can provide a sense of security and belonging, as well as opportunities for connection and emotional support. Building and maintaining healthy relationships can also help improve self-esteem and reduce feelings of loneliness and isolation.

In addition to self-care and building relationships, practicing mindfulness and stress management techniques can also help promote mental and emotional well-being. Mindfulness involves being present in the moment and paying attention to your thoughts and feelings without judgment. This can help reduce stress, anxiety, and depression, as well as improve focus and concentration.

Engaging in activities that bring you joy and fulfillment can also promote mental and emotional well-being. This could include pursuing hobbies, spending time in nature, volunteering, or practicing creativity. Doing things that you enjoy can boost your mood, increase your sense of purpose and meaning, and help you build resilience in the face of challenges.

It is important to remember that promoting mental and emotional well-being is an ongoing process that requires attention and effort. It is normal to experience ups and downs in your mental health, and seeking help when needed is a sign of strength, not weakness. There are a variety of resources available, including therapy, support groups, hotlines, and online resources, that can provide support and guidance during difficult times. By practicing self-care, building relationships, practicing mindfulness, engaging in activities that bring joy, and seeking help when needed, you can take steps to improve your mental and emotional health and create a more balanced and positive life.

Chapter 11: Recognizing and Addressing Substance Abuse

- IDENTIFYING SIGNS of substance abuse in teens

Substance abuse among teenagers is a growing concern in society. It is crucial for parents, educators, and healthcare professionals to be able to identify signs of substance abuse early on in order to intervene and provide necessary support and care for the affected individual. Adolescence is a time of experimentation and peer influence, and teenagers may be more likely to engage in risky behaviors, including substance abuse. By being aware of the signs and symptoms of substance abuse, adults can help prevent long-term consequences and provide appropriate resources for those in need.

One of the key signs of substance abuse in teens is a sudden change in behavior and mood. If a teenager who was once outgoing and social suddenly becomes withdrawn or irritable, it could be a red flag that they are struggling with substance abuse. Additionally, a decline in academic performance, loss of interest in hobbies or activities they once enjoyed, and changes in sleep patterns can also be indicators of substance abuse. It is important for parents and caregivers to pay attention to these changes and be proactive in addressing them with the teenager.

Physical signs of substance abuse in teens can also be present and should not be ignored. These can include bloodshot eyes, dilated or constricted pupils, sudden weight loss or gain, and unexplained injuries or bruises. It is important for adults to be observant of these physical signs and seek medical attention if necessary. Additionally, a teenager may exhibit changes in their hygiene and grooming habits, neglecting their personal appearance. These changes can be indicative of substance abuse and should be addressed promptly.

Another important sign of substance abuse in teens is a sudden change in social circle or peer group. Adolescents are heavily influenced by their peers, and a sudden shift in friendships can be a warning sign that the teenager is engaging in risky behavior, such as substance abuse. It is crucial for parents and caregivers to be aware of the teenager's social interactions and to communicate openly with them about their friendships and activities. By fostering a supportive and open relationship with the teenager, adults can help prevent substance abuse and provide guidance and support when needed.

In addition to behavioral, physical, and social signs of substance abuse, adults should also be aware of the emotional signs that may indicate a teenager is struggling with substance abuse. These can include increased irritability, mood swings, anxiety, and depression. Teenagers may also exhibit changes in their personality, such as increased impulsivity or aggression. It is important for adults to be sensitive to these emotional changes and to provide a safe and supportive environment for the teenager to express their feelings and concerns. Seeking professional help from a counselor or therapist can also be beneficial in addressing emotional issues related to substance abuse.

It is important for adults to approach the topic of substance abuse with sensitivity and compassion. Teenagers may feel ashamed or embarrassed about their substance abuse and may be hesitant to seek help. By creating a nonjudgmental and supportive environment, adults can help the teenager feel more comfortable discussing their struggles and seeking the necessary help and resources. It is important to listen actively to the teenager's concerns and to provide encouragement and support throughout the recovery process. Building trust and rapport with the teenager is crucial in helping them overcome substance abuse and work towards a healthier and more fulfilling future. By being aware of behavioral, physical, social, and emotional signs of substance abuse, adults can intervene early and provide the necessary support and care for teenagers in need. It is important for parents, educators, and healthcare professionals to work together to create a safe and supportive environment for teenagers to discuss their struggles and seek help. By approaching the topic of substance abuse with sensitivity and compassion, adults can help teenagers overcome their challenges and lead healthier and happier lives.

- Strategies for addressing substance abuse issues

Substance abuse is a complex and challenging issue that affects millions of individuals worldwide. It can have devastating effects on individuals, families, and communities, leading to physical and mental health problems, social and legal issues, and economic burdens. Addressing substance abuse requires a multifaceted approach that involves prevention, intervention, treatment, and ongoing support. In order to effectively address substance abuse issues, it is important to understand the underlying factors that contribute to substance abuse, as well as the various strategies that can be employed to prevent and treat it.

Prevention is a key component of addressing substance abuse issues. Prevention strategies aim to reduce the risk factors that contribute to substance abuse, as well as increase protective factors that can help individuals avoid substance abuse. Prevention efforts can take many forms, including education and awareness campaigns, school-based programs, community initiatives, and policy changes. By promoting healthy lifestyles, building coping skills, fostering positive relationships, and providing alternatives to substance use, prevention programs can help individuals make healthier choices and avoid the pitfalls of substance abuse.

Intervention is another critical element in addressing substance abuse. Intervention strategies aim to identify individuals who are at risk for or already engaging in substance abuse, and provide them with the necessary support and resources to address their issues. Early intervention is particularly important, as it can help prevent substance abuse from escalating and causing further harm. Intervention strategies can include screening and assessment, brief interventions, referral to treatment, and crisis intervention. By identifying individuals in need of help and connecting them to appropriate services, intervention programs can help individuals overcome their substance abuse issues before they become more serious.

Treatment is an essential component of addressing substance abuse issues. Treatment strategies aim to help individuals who are struggling with substance abuse to overcome their addiction, regain control of their lives, and make positive changes. Treatment can take many forms, including individual counseling, group therapy, medication-assisted treatment, detoxification, residential treatment, and outpatient programs. The goal of treatment is to address the physical, emotional, psychological, and social aspects of addiction, and help individuals develop the skills and resources they need to maintain their recovery in the long term. By providing comprehensive and personalized treatment, individuals can address the root causes of their substance abuse and learn to live healthier, happier lives.

Ongoing support is a crucial aspect of addressing substance abuse issues. Recovery from substance abuse is a lifelong journey, and individuals need ongoing support to maintain their sobriety and prevent relapse. Ongoing support can take many forms, including aftercare programs, support groups, peer counseling, mentoring, and follow-up care. By providing individuals with the tools, resources, and encouragement they need to stay on track with their recovery, ongoing support can help individuals overcome the challenges of addiction and build a strong foundation for a healthy, substance-free lifestyle. By understanding the underlying factors that contribute to substance abuse, as well as the strategies that can be employed to prevent and treat it, individuals, families, and communities can work together to overcome the challenges of addiction and build a brighter future. With the right resources, support, and determination, individuals struggling with substance abuse can achieve lasting recovery and live healthier, happier lives.

- Seeking professional help for addiction

Seeking professional help for addiction is a crucial step in the recovery process for individuals struggling with substance abuse. Addiction is a complex and chronic disease that can have devastating effects on a person's physical, mental, and emotional well-being. It is important to seek help from qualified professionals who have the knowledge and experience to provide effective treatment and support.

One of the main reasons why seeking professional help for addiction is so important is because addiction is a complex and multifaceted disease that requires specialized treatment. Professional addiction counselors and therapists have the training and expertise to assess each individual's unique needs and create a customized treatment plan that addresses their specific issues and challenges. They can provide evidence-based interventions, such as cognitive-behavioral therapy, motivational interviewing, and medication-assisted treatment, that have been proven to be effective in helping individuals overcome addiction.

In addition to providing personalized treatment plans, professional addiction counselors and therapists can also offer valuable support and guidance to individuals as they navigate the recovery process. Addiction can be a isolating and overwhelming experience, and having a supportive professional by your side can make a world of difference. Professional counselors and therapists can provide a safe and nonjudgmental space for individuals to share their thoughts and feelings, and can offer practical tools and strategies to help them cope with cravings, triggers, and other challenges that may arise during their recovery journey.

Another important aspect of seeking professional help for addiction is that it can help individuals to address any underlying issues that may be contributing to their substance abuse. Addiction is often fueled by a combination of genetic, environmental, and psychological factors, and professional counselors and therapists can help individuals to identify and process these underlying issues in order to prevent future relapse. For example, individuals may be using substances as a way to cope with trauma, stress, or mental health issues, and addressing these root causes is essential for long-term recovery.

Furthermore, seeking professional help for addiction can provide individuals with access to a wide range of resources and support services that can enhance their recovery experience. Professional counselors and therapists can connect individuals with support groups, community resources, and other treatment providers that can complement their treatment plan and provide additional avenues for support. They can also provide education and guidance on how to maintain a healthy and balanced lifestyle, develop healthy coping mechanisms, and build a strong support network to help prevent relapse. Professional counselors and therapists have the training, expertise, and resources to provide effective treatment and support that can help individuals overcome addiction and build a healthier, happier life. By seeking help from qualified professionals, individuals can receive personalized care, access evidence-based interventions, address underlying issues, and build a strong support network that can help them achieve long-term recovery and sobriety. If you or someone you know is struggling with addiction, do not hesitate to reach out to a professional counselor or therapist for help – it could make all the difference in your journey to recovery.

Chapter 12: Promoting Healthy Relationships

- UNDERSTANDING THE importance of healthy relationships

Healthy relationships are a crucial aspect of our overall well-being and quality of life. Whether it's with a romantic partner, family member, friend, or colleague, the relationships we foster and nurture have a significant impact on our physical, mental, and emotional health. Research has consistently shown that individuals who have strong, supportive relationships tend to experience lower levels of stress, anxiety, and depression, as well as improved physical health outcomes such as reduced risk of heart disease and better immune function.

One of the key benefits of healthy relationships is the sense of connection and belonging they provide. Feeling understood, valued, and supported by others helps us to develop a sense of belonging and community, which in turn contributes to our overall sense of well-being and happiness. When we have people in our lives who we can trust and rely on, we are more likely to feel secure and confident in ourselves, which can lead to greater self-esteem and resilience in the face of adversity.

Another important aspect of healthy relationships is the mutual give-and-take of support and care. In healthy relationships, both parties feel equally valued and respected, and they are able to communicate openly and honestly with each other. This creates a sense of equality and reciprocity, where both individuals feel that their needs and feelings are being heard and validated. This type of relationship dynamic fosters a sense of trust and collaboration, which can lead to increased feelings of intimacy and closeness between partners.

Healthy relationships also play a crucial role in our ability to effectively manage stress and cope with life's challenges. When we have a strong support system in place, we are better equipped to deal with difficult situations and navigate through times of crisis. Having someone to lean on during times of stress can help to reduce feelings of isolation and helplessness, and can provide us with a sense of comfort and reassurance. This type of emotional support can be invaluable in helping us to maintain our mental and emotional well-being during challenging times.

Furthermore, healthy relationships can have a positive impact on our physical health as well. Studies have shown that individuals in strong, supportive relationships are less likely to experience chronic health conditions such as heart disease, high blood pressure, and obesity. This is largely due to the fact that having someone to share our lives with can help to reduce feelings of loneliness and isolation, which in turn can have a positive effect on our overall health and well-being. Additionally, having a supportive partner or social network can encourage healthy behaviors such as regular exercise, a balanced diet, and getting enough sleep, all of which contribute to better physical health outcomes. They provide us with a sense of connection and belonging, mutual support and care, and the ability to effectively manage stress and cope with life's challenges. Cultivating and nurturing healthy relationships can have a profound impact on our physical, mental, and emotional health, leading to improved overall well-being and a greater sense of fulfillment and happiness in our lives. It is important to prioritize building and maintaining healthy relationships in our lives, as they are essential to our happiness and overall well-being.

- Teaching teens about consent and boundaries

Teaching teens about consent and boundaries is a critical aspect of their overall development and well-being. It is essential for young people to understand the importance of respecting others' boundaries and obtaining consent in all aspects of their lives, including relationships, friendships, and interactions with peers. By educating teens about these concepts, we can help them navigate social situations more effectively and empower them to make informed decisions about their own bodies and boundaries.

Consent is a fundamental concept that underpins all healthy relationships and interactions. It is the act of giving permission for something to happen, whether that be physical contact, sharing personal information, or engaging in a particular activity. Teaching teens about consent involves helping them understand that it is essential to seek and receive explicit permission from others before engaging in any form of physical or emotional intimacy. This includes recognizing and respecting non-verbal cues, such as body language or facial expressions, that indicate discomfort or unwillingness to participate in a particular activity.

Setting and respecting boundaries is another crucial aspect of teaching teens about consent. Boundaries are the limits that individuals set for themselves in order to protect their physical, emotional, and mental well-being. By encouraging teens to establish and communicate their boundaries clearly, we can help them assert their autonomy and self-worth in various relationships. It is important for teens to understand that it is okay to say no to something that makes them uncomfortable or goes against their values, and that they have the right to advocate for their own needs and well-being.

In order to effectively teach teens about consent and boundaries, it is important to engage them in open and honest conversations about these topics. Creating a safe and non-judgmental environment where teens feel comfortable discussing their thoughts and experiences can help facilitate meaningful discussions about consent and boundaries. Providing teens with accurate and age-appropriate information about these concepts can empower them to make informed decisions about their relationships and interactions with others. It is also essential to address common misconceptions and myths surrounding consent and boundaries, such as the belief that consent is not necessary in certain situations or that ignoring someone's boundaries is acceptable behavior.

In addition to verbal discussions, it can be helpful to incorporate interactive exercises and activities that promote understanding and awareness of consent and boundaries. Role-playing scenarios, watching and discussing relevant media content, and participating in group discussions can all be effective ways to engage teens in learning about these important topics. By encouraging active participation and reflection, we can help teens internalize the principles of consent and boundaries and apply them to their own lives.

It is also crucial to address the role of peer pressure and societal norms in shaping teens' attitudes towards consent and boundaries. In many social contexts, there can be pressure to conform to certain expectations or norms, which can make it challenging for teens to assert their boundaries and advocate for consent. By promoting critical thinking and self-awareness, we can empower teens to challenge harmful beliefs and behaviors that undermine their autonomy and well-being. Encouraging teens to surround themselves with supportive and respectful individuals who value consent and boundaries can also help create a positive and inclusive social environment. By promoting awareness, understanding, and respect for these concepts, we can empower teens to navigate relationships and interactions with confidence and autonomy. By fostering open and honest conversations, providing accurate information, and promoting critical thinking, we can help teens build healthy and respectful relationships with others and advocate for their own needs and boundaries. Through education and support, we can create a culture of consent and respect that benefits individuals and communities alike.

- Addressing issues of dating violence and abuse

Dating violence and abuse is a complex and multi-faceted issue that affects individuals of all ages, genders, and backgrounds. It is important to note that dating violence can take many forms, including physical, emotional, verbal, sexual, and financial abuse. This type of abuse can have a devastating impact on a person's physical and emotional well-being, as well as their overall quality of life. In order to address the issue of dating violence and abuse, it is crucial to understand the underlying causes and risk factors that contribute to this type of behavior.

One of the key risk factors for dating violence is a history of childhood trauma or abuse. Research has shown that individuals who have experienced abuse or trauma in their past are more likely to perpetrate violence in their relationships as adults. Additionally, individuals who have witnessed or experienced violence in their own families are at a higher risk of becoming victims or perpetrators of dating violence. These early life experiences can shape a person's attitudes and beliefs about relationships, power dynamics, and conflict resolution, leading to unhealthy and abusive behavior.

Another important risk factor for dating violence is gender inequality and traditional gender norms. Societal expectations around gender roles and behaviors can contribute to power imbalances in relationships, which can in turn lead to abuse. For example, men are often socialized to believe that they should be dominant, aggressive, and in control, while women are socialized to be submissive, passive, and nurturing. These rigid gender expectations can create toxic dynamics in relationships where one partner feels entitled to control or dominate the other, using violence as a means of asserting power and control.

It is also important to recognize that dating violence and abuse can occur in same-sex relationships, as well as heterosexual relationships. LGBTQ individuals may face additional challenges when seeking help for dating violence, as they may fear discrimination or lack access to culturally competent services. It is crucial for service providers and advocates to be inclusive and affirming of all identities and experiences when addressing dating violence, and to ensure that all individuals have access to supportive resources and services.

In order to effectively address issues of dating violence and abuse, it is essential to raise awareness and educate individuals about healthy relationships and boundaries. Prevention efforts should focus on promoting respectful communication, consent, and mutual respect in relationships, as well as providing resources and support for individuals who may be experiencing abuse. Schools, community organizations, and health care providers can play a key role in teaching young people about healthy relationships and empowering them to recognize and respond to signs of abuse.

Furthermore, it is important for society as a whole to challenge harmful attitudes and beliefs about gender and power that contribute to dating violence. This includes promoting gender equality, challenging stereotypes, and fostering open dialogue about healthy relationships and consent. By creating a culture of respect and empowerment, we can work towards preventing dating violence and promoting the well-being of all individuals in relationships. By working together to promote respect, equality, and safety in relationships, we can create a society where dating violence is no longer tolerated and all individuals are able to thrive in healthy and fulfilling partnerships.

Chapter 13: Supporting Academic Success

- STRATEGIES FOR SUPPORTING academic achievement in teens

As adolescents navigate the complex and challenging world of academia, it is important for educators, parents, and mentors to implement strategies that support their academic achievement. This crucial period in a teenager's life is marked by significant cognitive, emotional, and social development, making it essential to provide them with the right tools and resources to succeed academically. By implementing effective strategies for supporting academic achievement in teens, we can help them reach their full potential and set them on a path towards a successful future.

One of the key strategies for supporting academic achievement in teens is to create a supportive and nurturing environment. This includes fostering a positive and encouraging atmosphere at home, school, and in the community. Parents, teachers, and other caregivers play a vital role in creating this environment by providing teens with the necessary support, guidance, and encouragement to excel academically. By offering praise and recognition for their achievements, as well as providing them with the necessary resources and assistance when needed, we can help teens feel motivated and confident in their academic abilities.

Another important strategy for supporting academic achievement in teens is to set clear and realistic goals. By helping teens identify their academic strengths and weaknesses, as well as their long-term academic and career goals, we can assist them in creating a roadmap for success. Setting specific, measurable, achievable, relevant, and time-bound (SMART) goals can help teens stay focused and motivated, as well as track their progress and make adjustments as needed. By helping teens develop a clear vision of what they want to achieve academically, we can empower them to take control of their own learning and make informed decisions about their future.

In addition to creating a supportive environment and setting clear goals, it is essential to teach teens effective time management and study skills. Time management is a critical skill that can help teens juggle their academic responsibilities, extracurricular activities, and personal commitments. By encouraging teens to create a study schedule, prioritize tasks, and set aside dedicated time for studying, we can help them develop good habits that will serve them well throughout their academic career. Additionally, teaching teens effective study skills, such as note-taking, summarizing, and test-taking strategies, can help them improve their academic performance and excel in their coursework.

Furthermore, providing teens with access to academic resources and support services can also play a significant role in supporting their academic achievement. This includes offering tutoring, counseling, and academic advising services to assist teens in overcoming academic challenges and reaching their full potential. Additionally, providing teens with access to educational technology, such as online resources, interactive learning tools, and educational apps, can help them engage with their coursework and enhance their understanding of challenging concepts. By giving teens the resources and support they need to succeed academically, we can help them build confidence, develop critical thinking skills, and achieve their academic goals. By implementing these strategies, we can help teens navigate the challenges of academia and reach their full potential. It is crucial for educators, parents, and mentors to work together to empower teens to succeed academically and set them on a path towards a bright and successful future. By investing in the academic success of our teens, we are investing in the future of our society as a whole.

- Encouraging a positive attitude towards learning

Encouraging a positive attitude towards learning is essential for students to reach their full potential and achieve academic success. When students have a positive attitude towards learning, they are more likely to be motivated, engaged, and persistent in their studies. This positive attitude can lead to improved academic performance, increased confidence, and a lifelong love of learning.

One of the most effective ways to encourage a positive attitude towards learning is to create a supportive and inclusive learning environment. This can be achieved by fostering positive relationships between students and teachers, providing opportunities for collaboration and feedback, and recognizing and celebrating student achievements. When students feel supported and valued in the classroom, they are more likely to approach learning with a positive attitude.

Another important aspect of encouraging a positive attitude towards learning is to help students set realistic goals and expectations for themselves. By setting achievable goals and breaking them down into manageable tasks, students can build confidence in their abilities and track their progress over time. Celebrating small victories along the way can also help students stay motivated and engaged in their learning.

In addition to setting goals, it is important to help students develop a growth mindset. A growth mindset is the belief that intelligence and abilities can be developed through effort and persistence. When students have a growth mindset, they are more likely to embrace challenges, learn from their mistakes, and seek out feedback to improve. By promoting a growth mindset in the classroom, teachers can help students cultivate a positive attitude towards learning.

It is also important for educators to create a curriculum that is engaging, relevant, and challenging for students. When students are presented with interesting and meaningful content, they are more likely to be motivated to learn and actively participate in their studies. By incorporating real-world examples, hands-on activities, and project-based learning into the curriculum, teachers can help students see the practical applications of their learning and stay engaged in their studies.

Furthermore, it is essential for educators to provide regular and constructive feedback to students. Feedback allows students to understand their strengths and areas for improvement, and helps them track their progress towards their goals. By providing specific, timely, and actionable feedback, teachers can help students develop a growth mindset and continuously improve their learning. Encouraging students to reflect on their feedback and make adjustments to their learning strategies can further foster a positive attitude towards learning. By creating a supportive and inclusive learning environment, helping students set realistic goals and develop a growth mindset, providing engaging and challenging content, and offering regular and constructive feedback, educators can help students cultivate a positive attitude towards learning. With a positive attitude, students can overcome challenges, persist in their studies, and ultimately reach their full potential.

- Addressing challenges related to school performance

School performance is a crucial aspect of a student's academic journey, as it directly impacts their future opportunities and success. However, many students face challenges that can hinder their performance in school. These challenges can range from personal issues to academic difficulties, and they require proactive intervention in order to address them effectively. In this essay, we will explore some of the most common challenges related to school performance and discuss strategies that can be implemented to support students in overcoming these obstacles.

One of the most common challenges that students face in relation to school performance is a lack of motivation. It is not uncommon for students to feel demotivated and disengaged from their studies, especially when they do not see the relevance of what they are learning to their future goals. This lack of motivation can lead to poor attendance, incomplete assignments, and ultimately lower academic achievement. In order to address this challenge, it is important for educators to help students connect their learning to real-world applications and show them how their academic efforts can contribute to their personal and professional growth.

Another common challenge related to school performance is a lack of support at home. Many students come from disadvantaged backgrounds or unstable family situations, which can impact their ability to focus on their studies. Without a strong support system at home, students may struggle to stay organized, complete assignments, and manage their time effectively. In these cases, it is important for educators to provide additional support and resources to help students navigate these challenges. This can include connecting students with community resources, offering counseling services, or providing after-school tutoring programs.

In addition to motivation and support, academic challenges can also impact a student's school performance. Some students may struggle with specific subjects or concepts, leading to feelings of frustration and inadequacy. This can result in lower grades, decreased confidence, and a lack of interest in learning. In order to address academic challenges, it is essential for educators to identify areas of weakness and provide targeted interventions to support student learning. This can include offering extra help sessions, personalized tutoring, or modified assignments to accommodate different learning styles.

Furthermore, students may face social and emotional challenges that impact their school performance. Bullying, peer pressure, and mental health issues can all have a significant impact on a student's well-being and ability to succeed academically. It is important for educators to create a safe and supportive school environment that promotes positive relationships and open communication. By fostering a sense of belonging and community, students are more likely to feel motivated, engaged, and supported in their academic pursuits.

One of the key strategies for addressing challenges related to school performance is building strong relationships between educators, students, and families. By creating a collaborative and inclusive learning environment, students are more likely to feel supported and empowered to overcome obstacles. Educators can communicate regularly with parents and caregivers to ensure that they are aware of any challenges their child may be facing and can work together to develop a plan for success. Additionally, educators can cultivate positive relationships with students by showing empathy, understanding, and respect for their unique needs and strengths.

Another effective strategy for addressing challenges related to school performance is providing targeted interventions and support services. This can include academic counseling, mental health resources, and personalized learning plans to address individual student needs. Educators can work with school counselors, social workers, and other support staff to identify students who may be at risk and provide them with the necessary resources and interventions to help them succeed. By offering a range of support services, schools can create a more inclusive and equitable learning environment that meets the diverse needs of all students. By recognizing the unique needs and strengths of each student and providing targeted interventions and support services, educators can help students overcome obstacles and achieve their full potential. Through building strong relationships, fostering a positive school culture, and providing personalized support, schools can create an inclusive and supportive learning environment where all students can thrive academically and socially.

Chapter 14: Navigating Technology Use

- UNDERSTANDING THE impact of technology on teen behavior

The impact of technology on teen behavior is a widely studied and debated topic in today's society. With the rise of smartphones, social media, and constant connectivity, teenagers are increasingly relying on technology for communication, entertainment, and information. While technology has undoubtedly brought many benefits to teenagers, such as instant access to knowledge and the ability to connect with friends and family across the globe, it has also raised concerns about the negative effects it may have on their behavior.

One of the most significant impacts of technology on teen behavior is the prevalence of screen time and its potential negative effects on mental health. Studies have shown that excessive screen time, particularly on social media platforms, can lead to feelings of loneliness, anxiety, and depression. Teenagers are constantly bombarded with images and messages that portray an idealized version of life, leading to feelings of inadequacy and low self-esteem. This, in turn, can lead to risky behaviors such as cyberbullying, online harassment, and even self-harm.

Additionally, technology has also been shown to impact teenagers' cognitive development and attention span. The constant stimulation and multitasking required by technology can make it difficult for teenagers to focus and concentrate on one task at a time. This can lead to problems with memory retention, critical thinking, and problem-solving skills. Furthermore, the instant gratification provided by technology can lead to a decrease in patience and perseverance, as teenagers become accustomed to getting what they want with the click of a button.

On a more positive note, technology has also had a positive impact on teen behavior in many ways. For example, social media platforms have provided teenagers with a platform to express themselves creatively, connect with like-minded individuals, and pursue their interests and hobbies. Technology has also made it easier for teenagers to access educational resources and information, allowing them to expand their knowledge and skills in ways that were not possible before. While technology has brought many benefits to teenagers, such as instant access to information and the ability to connect with others, it has also raised concerns about its potential negative effects on mental health, cognitive development, and attention span. It is important for parents, educators, and policymakers to be mindful of these potential risks and work together to ensure that teenagers are using technology in a healthy and responsible manner. By promoting digital literacy, encouraging positive online behaviors, and providing support and guidance when needed, we can help teenagers navigate the challenges of the digital age and harness the full potential of technology for their personal and academic growth.

- Setting limits and boundaries for screen time

In today's digital age, screen time has become an increasingly prevalent aspect of daily life for people of all ages. The rise of smartphones, tablets, computers, and other electronic devices has made it easier than ever to be constantly connected to the online world. While these technological advancements have brought about many benefits in terms of communication, education, and entertainment, they have also raised concerns about the potential negative impacts of excessive screen time on individuals' physical and mental well-being.

Setting limits and boundaries for screen time is an important aspect of promoting healthy and balanced use of electronic devices. Research has shown that excessive screen time can have detrimental effects on various aspects of health, including sleep, mental health, and physical well-being. For example, spending prolonged periods of time in front of screens can disrupt circadian rhythms and interfere with the body's natural sleep-wake cycle, leading to sleep disturbances and insomnia. Additionally, excessive screen time has been linked to an increased risk of developing mental health issues such as anxiety and depression, as well as physical health problems such as obesity and eye strain.

In order to mitigate these potential negative consequences, it is crucial for individuals to establish clear limits and boundaries for their screen time usage. This can involve setting specific time limits for how long electronic devices can be used each day, as well as creating designated screen-free zones in the home or workplace. By establishing these boundaries, individuals can help ensure that they are engaging in a healthy and balanced relationship with technology, rather than allowing it to consume their lives.

One strategy for setting limits on screen time is to prioritize activities that promote physical activity and social interaction. Engaging in regular exercise, spending time outdoors, and participating in face-to-face interactions with friends and family can help reduce the amount of time spent in front of screens. By incorporating these types of activities into daily routines, individuals can not only limit their screen time but also improve their overall health and well-being.

Another important aspect of setting boundaries for screen time is to establish clear rules and expectations around device usage within the family or household. This can involve creating a family media plan that outlines when and where electronic devices can be used, as well as the types of content that are appropriate for different age groups. By involving all family members in the development of these guidelines, parents can help promote responsible and healthy screen time habits among children and adolescents.

In addition to setting limits on screen time, it is also important for individuals to be mindful of the quality of their screen time activities. Not all screen time is created equal, and certain types of content and interactions can have a more positive impact on mental and emotional well-being than others. For example, engaging in educational activities, creative pursuits, and meaningful social connections online can be beneficial for individuals, whereas mindlessly scrolling through social media or playing violent video games may have more negative effects.

Ultimately, setting limits and boundaries for screen time is about finding a balance between the benefits and drawbacks of technology in our lives. By being mindful of the amount and quality of screen time that we engage in, and by establishing clear guidelines and expectations for ourselves and our families, we can help ensure that technology remains a positive and enriching aspect of our lives, rather than a source of stress or harm. By prioritizing activities that promote physical, mental, and emotional well-being, and by fostering healthy relationships with technology, we can create a more balanced and fulfilling way of living in the digital age.

- Promoting healthy technology habits

In today's digital age, technology plays an integral role in our daily lives. From smartphones and laptops to smart TVs and wearable devices, we are constantly surrounded by technology. While technology has brought about many benefits and advancements, it is important to be mindful of our technology habits and ensure that they promote our overall well-being. Promoting healthy technology habits involves creating a balance between our screen time, ensuring that we are using technology in a way that enhances our lives rather than detracts from it.

One key aspect of promoting healthy technology habits is being mindful of the amount of time we spend on our devices. With the rise of social media, streaming services, and online gaming, it can be easy to get sucked into the digital world and spend hours mindlessly scrolling through feeds or binge-watching shows. However, excessive screen time has been linked to a variety of negative health effects, including eye strain, headaches, sleep disturbances, and decreased physical activity. By setting limits on our screen time and taking regular breaks from our devices, we can reduce the negative impact of excessive screen time on our health and well-being.

Another important aspect of promoting healthy technology habits is being intentional about how we use technology. Rather than using our devices as a means of escaping from reality or filling up idle time, we should strive to use technology in ways that enhance our lives and support our goals. This could involve using technology to stay connected with loved ones, learn new skills or information, or engage in hobbies and activities that bring us joy. By being intentional about how we use technology, we can ensure that our technology habits are contributing to our overall well-being rather than detracting from it.

In addition to being mindful of our screen time and intentional about how we use technology, promoting healthy technology habits also involves creating boundaries around our technology use. This could involve setting designated times when we are allowed to use our devices, such as turning off screens an hour before bedtime to promote better sleep or designating tech-free zones in our homes, such as the dinner table or bedroom. By creating boundaries around our technology use, we can prevent technology from taking over our lives and ensure that we are able to maintain a healthy balance between our digital and offline worlds.

In closing, promoting healthy technology habits also involves practicing good digital hygiene. This includes implementing strategies to protect our privacy and security online, such as using strong passwords, enabling two-factor authentication, and being cautious about what information we share online. It also involves being mindful of the content we consume online and being critical of the sources of information we encounter. By practicing good digital hygiene, we can ensure that our technology habits are not only healthy for us individually but also for our broader digital community. By being mindful of our screen time, intentional about how we use technology, creating boundaries around our technology use, and practicing good digital hygiene, we can ensure that our technology habits are supporting our overall well-being rather than detracting from it. By taking a proactive and intentional approach to our technology use, we can harness the many benefits of technology while minimizing its negative effects on our health and well-being. It is important for individuals, families, and communities to prioritize healthy technology habits and strive to create a balanced and mindful relationship with technology in order to thrive in today's digital world.

Chapter 15: Building a Supportive Community

- ENGAGING WITH SCHOOLS, communities, and resources

Engaging with schools, communities, and resources is a crucial aspect of creating a positive and impactful learning environment for students. This collaborative approach fosters a sense of community and teamwork, ultimately benefiting everyone involved.

Schools play a central role in engaging with students, families, and the broader community. By creating partnerships with local schools, educators can gain valuable insights into the needs and interests of their students, as well as access to resources and support services that can enhance the learning experience. Collaborating with schools also provides opportunities for educators to exchange ideas and best practices, ultimately improving teaching and learning outcomes.

Community engagement is another key aspect of creating a supportive learning environment. By reaching out to local organizations, businesses, and community members, educators can enrich the educational experience for their students. Community partnerships can provide students with real-world learning opportunities, such as internships, mentorships, and service projects, that enhance their understanding of the world around them. Engaging with the community also fosters a sense of belonging and connection, creating a supportive network of individuals who are invested in the success of the students.

In addition to schools and communities, resources such as libraries, museums, and online educational platforms can play a vital role in enhancing the learning experience. These resources offer educators access to a wealth of information and materials that can supplement their curriculum and engage students in new and exciting ways. By incorporating resources into their teaching practices, educators can create dynamic and interactive learning experiences that cater to the diverse needs and interests of their students. This collaborative approach not only benefits students, but also strengthens the educational system as a whole, creating a supportive network of individuals who are dedicated to the success of the next generation.

- Creating a network of support for teens

Creating a network of support for teens is crucial in today's society, as the teenage years can be a challenging and tumultuous time for many young individuals. This period of life is marked by significant physical, emotional, and social changes, and teens often face a myriad of issues such as academic pressure, peer relationships, self-esteem, identity formation, and mental health concerns. In order to help teens navigate these challenges and thrive during their adolescent years, it is essential to establish a strong support system that can offer guidance, resources, and encouragement. By building a network of support for teens, we can enhance their overall well-being, resilience, and successful transition into adulthood.

One key element of creating a network of support for teens is fostering positive relationships with parents, caregivers, teachers, mentors, counselors, and other adults in their lives. Research has shown that strong connections with supportive adults can have a significant impact on teens' emotional and psychological well-being, academic achievement, and overall development. These relationships can provide teens with a sense of security, stability, and trust, as well as opportunities for guidance, constructive feedback, and mentorship. By nurturing these relationships, adults can help teens build resilience, cope with stress, and develop essential life skills that will serve them well in the future.

In addition to adult relationships, peer support is also a crucial component of a strong network for teens. Peer relationships play a central role in adolescents' social and emotional development, as teens often rely on their friends for companionship, validation, and support. Positive peer relationships can offer teens a sense of belonging, acceptance, and camaraderie, as well as opportunities to learn from one another, share experiences, and explore new interests. By promoting a culture of inclusivity, respect, and empathy among peers, we can create a supportive environment that fosters healthy friendships, emotional well-being, and positive social interactions among teens.

Furthermore, creating a network of support for teens involves providing access to mental health resources, counseling services, and other professional supports to address the unique challenges and needs of adolescents. Research has shown that mental health issues such as anxiety, depression, and substance abuse are increasingly prevalent among teens, with a significant impact on their emotional well-being, academic performance, and overall quality of life. By offering comprehensive mental health services, early intervention, and support to teens in need, we can promote positive mental health outcomes, reduce stigma, and increase access to care for vulnerable youth. By fostering positive relationships with adults and peers, providing access to mental health resources, and promoting a culture of inclusivity and empathy, we can support teens in navigating the challenges of adolescence and thriving during this critical period of development. Through collaboration, communication, and community engagement, we can build a strong network of support that empowers teens to reach their full potential, build resilience, and lead healthy, fulfilling lives.

- Promoting a sense of belonging and connection

Belonging and connection are essential aspects of human well-being and flourishing. When individuals feel a sense of belonging, they feel accepted, valued, and included in a particular group or community. This sense of connection can lead to increased happiness, motivation, and overall life satisfaction. Unfortunately, many people struggle to find this sense of belonging in their lives, whether it be in their workplace, school, or social circles. It is crucial for individuals, organizations, and communities to prioritize and promote a sense of belonging and connection in order to create a supportive and inclusive environment for all.

One of the key ways to promote a sense of belonging and connection is through fostering strong relationships and connections with others. Building genuine and meaningful relationships with those around us can create a sense of belonging and community. This can be achieved through activities that encourage teamwork, collaboration, and communication. In a professional setting, team-building exercises, social events, and open communication channels can help foster a sense of connection among coworkers. Similarly, in a school or community setting, group projects, volunteer opportunities, and social activities can help individuals feel more connected to their peers and surroundings. By investing time and energy into building relationships with others, individuals can create a sense of belonging that can enhance their overall well-being.

Another important way to promote a sense of belonging and connection is through creating a welcoming and inclusive environment. This involves ensuring that all individuals feel accepted, valued, and respected in a particular setting. In a workplace, this can be achieved by promoting diversity and inclusion initiatives, creating a culture of respect and appreciation, and providing opportunities for employees to voice their opinions and ideas. In a school or community setting, this can involve promoting inclusivity, celebrating diversity, and creating spaces where individuals feel safe and supported. By creating an inclusive environment where everyone feels welcome and valued, individuals are more likely to develop a sense of belonging and connection to the group or community.

Furthermore, promoting a sense of belonging and connection can also involve providing support and resources for individuals to help them feel connected to a particular group or community. This may include offering mentorship programs, counseling services, or support groups for individuals who may be struggling to find their place or feel included. In a professional setting, this can involve providing opportunities for professional development, career advancement, and personal growth. In a school or community setting, this can involve offering academic support, mental health resources, and extracurricular activities that cater to the diverse needs of individuals. By providing support and resources for individuals, organizations and communities can help individuals feel more connected and supported, ultimately promoting a sense of belonging and connection. By fostering strong relationships, creating a welcoming and inclusive environment, and providing support and resources for individuals, organizations and communities can help individuals feel accepted, valued, and connected to their surroundings. Ultimately, a sense of belonging and connection can lead to increased happiness, motivation, and overall well-being for individuals. It is important for individuals, organizations, and communities to prioritize and promote a sense of belonging and connection in order to create a positive and supportive environment for all.

Chapter 16: Addressing Cultural and Diversity Issues

- RECOGNIZING THE INFLUENCE of culture on teen behavior

Teen behavior is shaped by a multitude of factors, one of the most significant being culture. Culture is defined as the beliefs, customs, and behaviors of a particular group of people, and it plays a crucial role in shaping how teenagers think, act, and interact with others. Recognizing the influence of culture on teen behavior is essential in understanding the complex dynamics that drive adolescent development and decision-making.

One way in which culture influences teen behavior is through the values and norms that are passed down from one generation to another. Different cultures place varying degrees of emphasis on traits such as independence, collectivism, respect for authority, and gender roles. These cultural values can significantly influence how teenagers perceive themselves and others, as well as how they navigate social relationships and expectations. For example, in some cultures, there may be a strong emphasis on obedience and deference to authority figures, which could shape how teens interact with teachers, parents, and other authority figures in their lives.

Additionally, culture also influences the attitudes and beliefs that teens hold about specific issues such as education, careers, relationships, and religion. Cultural norms can dictate the importance of academic achievement, the value of a traditional career path versus pursuing creative endeavors, the expectations around dating and marriage, and the role of spirituality in one's life. These cultural attitudes can shape how teenagers set goals for themselves, make decisions about their future, and navigate the challenges and opportunities that come their way.

Furthermore, culture plays a significant role in shaping how teenagers express their identity and navigate the complexities of adolescence. Cultural identity is a key aspect of self-concept for many teens, and it can impact how they view themselves, their peers, and their place in the world. For example, teenagers from immigrant families may straddle two cultures, negotiating the expectations and values of their family's cultural heritage with the pressures and influences of mainstream American culture. This balancing act can be a source of both strength and tension for teens, as they navigate the complexities of identity formation and belonging.

In addition to shaping individual attitudes and behaviors, culture also influences the social norms and practices that govern teen interactions and relationships. Different cultures have varying expectations around issues such as dating, friendships, family dynamics, and peer groups. For example, in some cultures, there may be strict rules around dating and courtship, with an emphasis on parental involvement and approval. In contrast, in other cultures, dating may be more casual and individualistic, with less emphasis on parental guidance. These cultural norms can shape how teens navigate their social lives, form friendships, and establish boundaries in their relationships.

Moreover, culture also plays a role in shaping how teens cope with challenges, setbacks, and stressors in their lives. Cultural beliefs and practices around mental health, resilience, and coping strategies can significantly impact how teenagers respond to adversity and seek support. For example, some cultures may stigmatize mental health issues and discourage seeking professional help, leading teens to internalize their struggles and avoid seeking the support they need. In contrast, other cultures may have more open attitudes towards mental health and encourage seeking help from trusted adults, peers, or mental health professionals. Culture shapes teens' values, beliefs, attitudes, identity, social interactions, and coping strategies in profound ways, influencing how they navigate the challenges and opportunities of adolescence. By taking into account the cultural context in which teenagers live and grow, educators, parents, and professionals can better support teens in their journey towards adulthood and foster a sense of belonging, resilience, and well-being.

- Fostering understanding and acceptance of diverse perspectives

In today's interconnected and diverse world, fostering understanding and acceptance of diverse perspectives is more crucial than ever. It is essential for individuals to recognize and appreciate different viewpoints, beliefs, and experiences in order to cultivate a more inclusive and harmonious society. By embracing diversity and learning from each other, we can break down barriers, challenge stereotypes, and build empathy and respect for one another.

One of the first steps in fostering understanding and acceptance of diverse perspectives is to recognize the inherent value and richness that come from different backgrounds and experiences. Each person brings a unique set of beliefs, values, and cultural practices to the table, which can enrich our collective understanding and broaden our horizons. By acknowledging and celebrating this diversity, we can create an environment where everyone feels respected, valued, and included.

Education plays a critical role in promoting understanding and acceptance of diverse perspectives. Schools, colleges, and universities have a unique opportunity to instill in students the importance of embracing diversity and engaging with different viewpoints. By incorporating diverse perspectives into curricula, facilitating open and respectful dialogue, and promoting cultural exchange programs, educational institutions can help students develop the skills and attitudes needed to thrive in a multicultural world.

Another key aspect of fostering understanding and acceptance of diverse perspectives is promoting open and respectful communication. By actively listening to others, asking questions, and seeking to understand different viewpoints, we can create meaningful connections and bridge perceived divides. It is important to approach discussions with an open mind, a willingness to learn, and a genuine curiosity about others' experiences. By engaging in honest and empathetic conversations, we can break down barriers, challenge assumptions, and build trust and mutual respect.

Building empathy is another crucial component of fostering understanding and acceptance of diverse perspectives. Empathy allows us to put ourselves in others' shoes, to understand their feelings, thoughts, and experiences, and to cultivate a deeper sense of connection and understanding. By practicing empathy, we can develop a greater appreciation for the similarities and differences that make us unique, and foster a greater sense of compassion and solidarity with others. By recognizing the value of diversity, promoting education and open communication, and cultivating empathy, we can bridge divides, challenge stereotypes, and create a more interconnected and empathetic world. It is up to each of us to do our part in embracing diversity, celebrating differences, and working towards a more just and inclusive society for all.

- Addressing issues of discrimination and bias

Discrimination and bias are pervasive issues that continue to impact individuals and communities across the globe. These forms of prejudice can manifest in various ways, including racism, sexism, homophobia, ableism, ageism, and more. Addressing these issues requires a multi-faceted approach that involves education, awareness, advocacy, and policy change. By examining the root causes of discrimination and bias, we can begin to dismantle the systems that perpetuate these harmful attitudes and behaviors.

One key aspect of addressing discrimination and bias is education. By raising awareness about the harmful effects of prejudice and promoting inclusivity and diversity, we can empower individuals to challenge their own biases and take action to create a more equitable society. Education can take many forms, from formal curriculum in schools to workplace training programs to community workshops and events. By providing individuals with the knowledge and tools they need to recognize and combat discrimination, we can begin to shift societal attitudes and behaviors towards a more inclusive and just society.

In addition to education, advocacy plays a crucial role in addressing discrimination and bias. Advocacy involves speaking out against injustice, standing up for marginalized communities, and working towards systemic change. By amplifying the voices of those who are most affected by discrimination and bias, advocates can help to bring about meaningful change at the individual, community, and societal levels. Advocacy can take many forms, from organizing protests and campaigns to lobbying for policy change to working to change cultural attitudes and norms. By working together to address discrimination and bias, advocates can help to create a more equitable and just society for all.

Policy change is another important aspect of addressing discrimination and bias. By enacting laws and policies that protect individuals from discrimination and promote diversity and inclusion, governments and organizations can help to create a more equitable society. This can include implementing anti-discrimination laws, creating diversity and inclusion initiatives, and ensuring that individuals have access to resources and support to address instances of discrimination. By taking a proactive approach to addressing discrimination and bias through policy change, we can help to create a more just and inclusive society for all.

It is also important to recognize the intersectionality of discrimination and bias. Intersectionality refers to the ways in which various forms of discrimination and bias intersect and compound to create unique experiences of oppression for individuals who hold multiple marginalized identities. For example, a Black woman may experience discrimination and bias differently than a white woman or a Black man, as she faces the combined forces of racism and sexism. By understanding and addressing the intersectionality of discrimination and bias, we can work towards creating more inclusive and equitable systems that uplift individuals of all backgrounds and identities. By working together to raise awareness, challenge harmful attitudes and behaviors, advocate for change, and enact policies that promote diversity and inclusion, we can create a more just and equitable society for all. It is incumbent upon all individuals to take a stand against discrimination and bias in their own lives and communities, and to work towards a world where everyone is treated with dignity and respect, regardless of their race, gender, sexual orientation, disability, age, or any other factor. By coming together to address these issues, we can create a more inclusive and equitable world for future generations.

Chapter 17: Planning for the Future

- ENCOURAGING TEENS to explore their interests and passions

Encouraging teenagers to explore their interests and passions is essential for their personal growth and development. Adolescence is a critical period in which individuals begin to discover who they are and what they are passionate about.

One way to encourage teenagers to explore their interests is to provide them with opportunities to try new things. This could involve enrolling them in extracurricular activities that align with their interests, such as sports, music, art, or volunteering. By exposing teenagers to a variety of activities, they can discover what they are passionate about and what they excel in. This can help them build confidence and self-esteem, as well as develop important skills such as teamwork, communication, and leadership.

Parents and educators play a crucial role in encouraging teenagers to explore their interests. By showing support and enthusiasm for their passions, parents can help teenagers feel validated and motivated to pursue their interests. Educators can also play a role in facilitating this process by creating a supportive environment in which teenagers feel encouraged to explore new ideas and try new things. By providing resources and guidance, educators can help teenagers discover their passions and cultivate their talents.

It is important to remember that exploring interests and passions is not just about finding a hobby or activity to pass the time. It is about discovering what truly excites and inspires an individual, and finding ways to incorporate that passion into their daily life. Encouraging teenagers to explore their interests can help them find fulfillment and purpose in their lives, leading to greater happiness and success in the long run.

One of the key benefits of encouraging teenagers to explore their interests is that it can help them develop a sense of identity and self-awareness. By allowing teenagers to explore different activities and experiences, they can learn more about themselves and what they are truly passionate about. This self-discovery process is crucial for teenagers as they navigate the complexities of adolescence and begin to shape their future goals and aspirations.

In addition to personal growth and self-awareness, exploring interests and passions can also have practical benefits for teenagers. By honing their skills and talents in areas of interest, teenagers can build a strong foundation for future success in their academic, professional, and personal lives. Whether it is pursuing a career in a field they are passionate about, or simply finding joy and fulfillment in a hobby or activity, exploring interests can help teenagers thrive in all areas of their lives. By providing them with opportunities to discover what truly excites and motivates them, we empower teenagers to develop their talents and skills, build confidence and self-esteem, and ultimately find fulfillment and success in their lives. Through the support of parents, educators, and mentors, teenagers can explore their interests, unlock their potential, and chart a path towards a bright and promising future.

- Supporting career exploration and educational goals

Supporting career exploration and educational goals is vital in helping individuals navigate their professional journeys and achieve success. By providing guidance, resources, and encouragement, individuals can make informed decisions about their future paths and pursue opportunities that align with their interests and skills. In this essay, we will explore the various ways in which individuals can be supported in their career exploration and educational goals, as well as the benefits of such support.

One of the key ways to support career exploration and educational goals is through mentorship. Mentors can provide valuable insight and advice to individuals as they navigate their career paths and make important decisions about their education and future. A mentor can help an individual identify their strengths and weaknesses, explore different career options, and develop a plan for achieving their goals. By sharing their own experiences and knowledge, a mentor can offer guidance and support that can help an individual make informed decisions and take steps towards their desired career path.

Another important way to support career exploration and educational goals is through networking. Building a strong professional network can provide individuals with valuable connections, resources, and opportunities to further their education and career goals. By connecting with professionals in their field of interest, individuals can gain insights into different career paths, learn about job opportunities, and establish relationships that can help them advance in their chosen field. Networking can also help individuals develop valuable skills such as communication, collaboration, and leadership, which are essential for success in today's competitive job market.

In addition to mentorship and networking, individuals can also benefit from career counseling services. Career counselors can provide individuals with guidance, resources, and support to help them identify their interests, strengths, and career goals. By working with a career counselor, individuals can explore different career options, develop a plan for achieving their goals, and overcome any challenges they may face along the way. Career counseling can also help individuals navigate the job search process, prepare for interviews, and build a strong resume and cover letter that highlights their skills and experience.

Furthermore, individuals can benefit from participating in career exploration programs and workshops. These programs can provide individuals with valuable information, resources, and support to help them discover their interests, explore different career options, and develop a plan for achieving their educational and career goals. By participating in these programs, individuals can gain valuable insights and experiences that can help them make informed decisions about their future and take steps towards their desired career path. These programs can also provide individuals with opportunities to connect with professionals in their field of interest, gain hands-on experience, and build valuable skills that can help them succeed in their chosen career. By providing mentorship, networking opportunities, career counseling services, and career exploration programs, individuals can gain valuable insights, resources, and support to help them make informed decisions about their future and pursue opportunities that align with their interests and skills. With the right support and guidance, individuals can overcome challenges, set and achieve their educational and career goals, and ultimately find success and fulfillment in their chosen fields.

- Helping teens navigate the transition to adulthood

Navigating the transition from adolescence to adulthood can be a challenging and confusing time for many teenagers. As they prepare to enter the adult world, they are faced with a myriad of decisions and responsibilities that they may not have had to deal with before. It is important for parents, educators, and other adults in their lives to provide support and guidance during this transitional period to help them successfully navigate this crucial stage of development.

One of the key components of helping teens navigate the transition to adulthood is providing them with the necessary skills and resources to make informed decisions. This includes teaching them about financial literacy, career planning, and healthy relationships. By equipping teens with these important life skills, they will be better prepared to take on the challenges of adulthood and make sound choices that will lead to a successful future.

In addition to providing practical skills, it is also important to offer emotional support and guidance to teens during this transitional period. Many teenagers may experience feelings of uncertainty, anxiety, and self-doubt as they navigate the transition to adulthood. It is important for adults to listen to their concerns, validate their feelings, and offer encouragement and reassurance. By providing a supportive and non-judgmental environment, adults can help teens build confidence and resilience as they navigate the ups and downs of growing up.

Another important aspect of helping teens transition to adulthood is fostering independence and autonomy. As teenagers begin to take on more responsibility and make decisions for themselves, it is important for adults to empower them to take ownership of their choices and actions. This can involve giving them opportunities to practice decision-making, problem-solving, and resourcefulness in a safe and supportive environment. By encouraging teens to think for themselves and take initiative, adults can help them develop the skills and confidence they need to navigate the challenges of adulthood.

In addition to providing practical skills and emotional support, it is also important for adults to help teens develop a sense of purpose and direction as they transition to adulthood. This can involve helping them explore their interests, passions, and values, and encouraging them to set goals and work towards achieving them. By helping teens identify their strengths and values, adults can support them in finding a sense of meaning and purpose in their lives. This can help teens develop a sense of identity and direction as they navigate the transition to adulthood.

To bring to a close, it is important for adults to be patient and understanding as teens navigate the transition to adulthood. Growing up is a complex and challenging process, and it is normal for teenagers to make mistakes, experience setbacks, and struggle with their emotions during this time. It is important for adults to offer support, guidance, and reassurance, even when things don't go as planned. By being patient and understanding, adults can help teens develop resilience, adaptability, and perseverance as they navigate the ups and downs of growing up. By providing practical skills, emotional support, autonomy, and purpose, adults can help teens build the confidence, resilience, and sense of direction they need to successfully transition to adulthood. By fostering a supportive and empowering environment, adults can help teens navigate this crucial stage of development with confidence and success.

Chapter 18: Conclusion

- RECAP OF KEY STRATEGIES for communication and connection with teens

Effective communication and connection with teens is essential for building strong relationships and facilitating positive outcomes in their lives. In today's fast-paced and technology-driven world, it can be challenging to connect with teenagers who are constantly bombarded with information and distractions. However, by employing key strategies and approaches, adults can bridge the communication gap and create meaningful connections with teens.

One of the most important strategies for effective communication with teens is active listening. This involves not only hearing what the teen is saying but also understanding their emotions, thoughts, and perspectives. Active listening requires adults to pay attention to verbal and non-verbal cues, respond empathetically, and validate the teen's feelings. By creating a safe and supportive environment for teens to express themselves, adults can foster trust and open communication.

Another key strategy for connecting with teens is to show genuine interest in their lives and activities. This involves asking open-ended questions, showing curiosity about their interests and hobbies, and actively participating in their activities when appropriate. By demonstrating interest in their lives, adults can show teens that they care about them as individuals and are invested in their well-being. This can help build rapport and strengthen the relationship between adults and teens.

Building trust is also crucial for effective communication with teens. Trust is the foundation of any relationship, and it is especially important for adults to earn the trust of teenagers. Adults can build trust with teens by being honest, reliable, and consistent in their words and actions. Trust is a two-way street, so adults must also trust teens and believe in their abilities and potential. By establishing trust, adults can create a safe and supportive environment for teens to open up and share their thoughts and feelings.

Setting boundaries and expectations is another important strategy for communicating with teens. Boundaries help establish clear guidelines for behavior and interactions, and expectations set the stage for positive outcomes. Adults should communicate boundaries and expectations clearly and consistently, and enforce them with fairness and empathy. By setting boundaries and expectations, adults can help teens understand their responsibilities and roles in the relationship, and promote mutual respect and understanding.

Effective communication with teens also involves being aware of cultural differences and individual differences. Teens come from diverse backgrounds and have unique experiences, beliefs, and values. By respecting and acknowledging cultural differences, adults can show teens that they value their perspectives and experiences. Similarly, by recognizing and accepting individual differences, adults can tailor their communication and approach to meet the needs and preferences of each teen. By being culturally competent and sensitive to individual differences, adults can create inclusive and welcoming environments for teens to thrive.

In summary, effective communication and connection with teens require adults to employ key strategies such as active listening, showing genuine interest, building trust, setting boundaries and expectations, and being aware of cultural and individual differences. By using these strategies, adults can build strong relationships with teens, foster open communication, and support positive outcomes in their lives. Ultimately, the goal of effective communication and connection with teens is to help them feel heard, valued, and supported, and to empower them to navigate the challenges of adolescence with confidence and resilience.

- **Final thoughts and reflections on teen behavior**

Teen behavior is a complex and multifaceted subject that has puzzled researchers, parents, and educators for generations. As adolescents navigate the turbulent waters of puberty and peer pressure, their behavior can often be confusing and challenging to understand. However, by taking a closer look at the underlying factors that influence teen behavior, we can gain a greater insight into why teenagers act the way they do.

One of the key factors that shape teen behavior is brain development. Teenagers are in the midst of a period of rapid brain growth and reorganization, particularly in the prefrontal cortex, which is responsible for decision-making, impulse control, and emotional regulation. This means that teens are more likely to engage in risky behaviors, such as experimentation with drugs and alcohol, without fully understanding the consequences of their actions. Additionally, the hormonal changes that occur during puberty can also contribute to mood swings and impulsive behavior in teenagers.

Peer influence is another significant factor that can impact teen behavior. As adolescents strive to establish their identity and fit in with their peers, they may be more susceptible to peer pressure and social norms. This can lead to behaviors such as bullying, clique formation, and risky behaviors in an effort to gain acceptance and approval from their peers. As such, it is essential for parents, teachers, and other influential adults in a teen's life to help guide and support them in making positive choices and resisting negative peer influences.

The family environment also plays a crucial role in shaping teen behavior. Family dynamics, communication patterns, and parenting styles can all impact a teen's behavior and emotional well-being. Research has shown that teens who have strong, supportive relationships with their parents are more likely to exhibit positive behaviors and make healthy choices. Conversely, teens who come from dysfunctional or neglectful family environments may be more prone to engaging in delinquent behaviors and struggling with mental health issues. It is important for parents to be actively involved in their teen's life, provide a supportive and nurturing environment, and set clear boundaries and expectations to help guide their behavior.

In addition to brain development, peer influence, and family dynamics, societal influences also play a role in shaping teen behavior. The media, popular culture, and social media can all impact how teenagers view themselves and others, as well as what behaviors they consider acceptable or desirable. Research has shown that exposure to violent or sexual content in the media can influence aggressive behavior in teenagers, while unrealistic body ideals portrayed in magazines and on social media can contribute to body image issues and low self-esteem. As such, it is important for parents, educators, and policymakers to be aware of the impact of these societal influences and work towards creating a more positive and empowering environment for teens. By understanding these underlying factors and working to create a supportive and nurturing environment for teenagers, we can help guide them towards making positive choices and developing into healthy, well-adjusted adults. It is essential for parents, teachers, and other adults in a teen's life to be actively involved, communicate openly and effectively, and provide guidance and support to help navigate the challenges of adolescence. With the right support and resources, teens can overcome the obstacles they face and thrive during this critical stage of development.

- Resources for further support and guidance

When seeking support and guidance in various areas of life, it is important to have access to a variety of resources that can provide assistance and assistance. Whether you are looking for help with mental health, career development, financial planning, or any other aspect of your life, there are a number of resources available to you. In this article, we will discuss some of the key resources that you can turn to for further support and guidance.

One of the most important resources for support and guidance is professional counseling. Counseling can provide you with a safe and supportive environment to explore your thoughts and feelings, and to work through any challenges or issues you may be facing. A trained counselor can help you gain insight into your thoughts and behaviors, and can provide you with tools and strategies to help you cope with difficult situations. Whether you are dealing with anxiety, depression, relationship issues, or any other mental health concern, counseling can be a valuable resource for support and guidance.

Another valuable resource for support and guidance is career counseling. Career counselors can help you explore your interests, skills, and values, and can assist you in identifying potential career paths that align with your goals and aspirations. They can also help you develop a plan for achieving your career objectives, whether that involves further education, networking, or other strategies. Career counseling can be particularly helpful if you are feeling stuck in your current job, or if you are unsure about what direction to take in your career.

Financial counseling is another important resource for support and guidance. A financial counselor can help you create a budget, set financial goals, and develop a plan for saving, investing, and managing your money. They can also provide you with information and resources to help you make informed decisions about your finances, such as understanding different types of loans or credit cards, or planning for retirement. Financial counseling can be particularly valuable if you are experiencing financial stress, or if you are unsure about how to manage your money effectively.

In addition to professional counseling, career counseling, and financial counseling, there are many other resources available for support and guidance in a variety of areas. Support groups, for example, can provide you with a community of people who are facing similar challenges and can offer understanding, advice, and encouragement. Whether you are dealing with a health condition, a relationship issue, a loss, or any other concern, a support group can be a valuable resource for finding comfort and connection.

Online resources can also be a valuable source of support and guidance. There are a variety of websites, forums, and social media platforms that offer information, advice, and support on a wide range of topics. Whether you are looking for therapy options, job search strategies, financial planning tools, or any other information, you can find it online. Many websites also offer resources for self-help, such as articles, videos, and worksheets that can help you develop new skills, improve your well-being, and achieve your goals. Whether you are seeking assistance with your mental health, career development, financial planning, or any other aspect of your life, there are professionals, organizations, and online platforms that can provide you with the help you need. By taking advantage of these resources, you can gain insight, build skills, and develop strategies to navigate life's challenges and achieve your goals. Remember, it is okay to ask for help, and there are many people and resources out there that are ready to support you on your journey.